What People Are Saying about Victor Torres Your Addicted Loved One...

"Victor Torres has given those with addicted loved ones practical tools to help them deal with the powerlessness they feel. This book is truly empowering and enlightening."

—*Bobby Schuller*
Pastor, *Hour of Power* on TBN

"I believe in miracles because I believe in God. I was standing at the entrance of the Teen Challenge Center with my wife, Gloria, when a young Victor Torres and his parents came looking for help. Victor was at the end of his rope, hanging by a thread, but then Jesus broke through and his life changed. Today, Victor is an authority on the subject of addiction. He has helped thousands find victory over addiction. This book tells it like it is, but even better, it imparts hope and change."

—*Nicky Cruz*
Founder, Nicky Cruz Outreach
Author, *Run Baby Run*

"If you have, or suspect you have, an addicted family member, read this book. Victor Torres will give you success steps for every part of this unwanted and challenging journey. You'll read the stories of others, find answers to your questions, and discover practical, tested principles you can apply to your own situation. This book is a valuable tool for families, churches, counselors, addiction recovery organizations, and leaders. Don't miss it!"

—*Carol Kent*
Speaker and Author of *When I Lay My Isaac Down*

"If you watch the news and look at the data, you know the truth: America is losing the war on drugs. We can't wait on government programs. The church needs to pull its head out of the sand and get its hands dirty in this fight—and Victor Torres provides the blueprint. Get this book for yourself or for a friend who is experiencing the hell of struggling to reach an addicted loved one. You may just save someone's life."

—*Pastor Sonny Arguinzoni*
Founder and President, Victory Outreach International

"We are all well aware of the prevalence and dangers of drug abuse, but this knowledge has failed to act as a deterrent. Heroin use and overdoses have skyrocketed, and more people are using and abusing prescription drugs than ever before. In *Reaching Your Addicted Loved One*, Victor Torres provides real-life advice along with plenty of successful testimonies of recovery to provide readers with hope. Let his many years of experience in helping thousands of addicts find their way to freedom give you the tools and hope you need to fight back."

—*Dr. Ed Hindson*
Evangelist and host of *The King Is Coming*
Dean and Distinguished Professor of Religion at Liberty University

REACHING YOUR

LOVED ONE

VICTOR TORRES

HELP & HOPE
FOR THOSE
BATTLING SUBSTANCE ABUSE

WHITAKER
HOUSE

REACHING YOUR ADDICTED LOVED ONE:
Help and Hope for Those Battling Substance Abuse

facebook.com/VictorTorresMinistries
newlifeforyouth.com

ISBN: 978-1-64123-100-8
eBook ISBN: 978-1-64123-101-5
Printed in the United States of America
© 2019 by Victor Torres

Whitaker House
1030 Hunt Valley Circle
New Kensington, PA 15068
www.whitakerhouse.com

Library of Congress Cataloging-in-Publication Data (Pending)

1 2 3 4 5 6 7 8 9 10 11 ⨆ 26 25 24 23 22 21 20 19

DEDICATION

To my beloved parents, Manuel and Adelayda Torres. I am still discovering what great parents you both were to me. Thank you for not giving up on me. You gave your best in your struggle and determination to fight for my life, finally bringing me to my breakthrough and victory over addiction.

ACKNOWLEDGMENTS

I would like to give a special thanks to a very talented and insightful editing team and to Suzanne Kuhn for your direction. Thanks to Lisa Eckman, Anita Agers, Arlene Moskwa, and my daughter, Rosalinda Rivera. Thank you for sharing the vision to reach our addicted loved ones.

CONTENTS

FOREWORD

This is a most timely and important book in light of today's drug epidemic. Both youth and adults are getting addicted to opioids and other drugs. Through his ministry, Victor Torres has helped thousands of people to be freed from drugs; he is well qualified to help parents and families that may be dealing with addiction in their immediate or extended family.

Addiction does not have to be a lifetime disease. Neither is it hopeless. *Reaching Your Addicted Loved One* is straight talk for those who want to help a young person or adult make the all-important decision to seek lasting help for addiction.

If you believe it's time to "take back" what drugs and addiction have stolen from you, I urge you to read this book. If you are so fortunate that addiction has not yet touched your family, then pass this book on to some parent or friend who may be at their wit's end.

There is an exit ramp off addiction's road to destruction. In these pages, you will find the vital road signs for how and where to find that exit.

—*Don Wilkerson*
President, Teen Challenge, Inc.

INTRODUCTION

Their desperate cries have echoed in my ears for more than half a century. The faces are different, but most of the questions and pleas are the same.

"How can I reach my child?" a mother or father asks.

"We've tried everything," a grandparent sobs.

"They keep promising something will change, but nothing ever does," a spouse laments.

Whether a parent, grandparent, spouse, sibling, extended family member, or close friend, all are expressing the depth of their fear. The stakes are real and the concern is valid. No wonder helplessness consumes them. It is evident by their plea: "I don't know what to do!"

Since you are reading this book, it is likely that you have a child, spouse, parent, sibling, or close friend who is caught in the web of drug or alcohol abuse. Or, perhaps you know someone else who is trying to help an addicted loved one. Whatever your reason for picking up this book, I can tell you firsthand: the helpless state of loving the addicted person is a terrible place to be. I don't make this statement because I have one in my life, but because I once *was* one.

For seven years, I used the needle. At the age of fourteen, I was a somewhat innocent kid who turned bad when I began using heroin. I took my first shot on a rooftop in Brooklyn, New York. A friend introduced it to me while four of us were hanging out together. I started off big, straight to mainlining, and from that first shot, I went downhill, fast.

My mother discovered my drug addiction the day I staggered into our little apartment. She instantly suspected something was grievously wrong. She grabbed my left arm, pulled up my sleeve, saw the needle marks, and screamed so loudly that they probably heard it down the street. "Oh my God, not this!"

I still remember the wide-eyed look of horror on her face. She had just seen the most horrible thing in her life. For me, it was nothing. I was under the influence and feeling no pain. But for my mother, it was the most awful agony she had ever experienced. She had seen the horrible effects that drug use had on other families—the look of death on the addicts and the devastating stories of mothers and fathers. She had hoped that we could avoid the kind of suffering that had stolen the peace and happiness of so many others. But because of me, she came face-to-face with the very thing she had feared most. Our turn had come.

Seldom are we taken by complete surprise when it comes to substance abuse. Our loved ones send us signals and clues throughout their addiction journey. Sometimes we fail to recognize them. Other times, we choose to look past them, desperately hoping we are wrong or that things will magically get better on their own.

It's difficult to describe the pain that people experience when they discover their loved one is addicted. The haunting questions that torment the mind can be as painful as the initial shock of discovery.

Where did I go wrong?

Is this my fault?

What do we do next?

Is this going to destroy our family?

Is there any hope at all for the future?

I have spoken in thousands of churches across the U.S., and without exception, no fewer than half the congregation raises their hands when I ask the burning question: How many of you have a loved one on drugs? Whether it is an inner-city neighborhood or a rural American community, the results are the same. Because I have a global ministry, I hear similar outcries from platforms around the world.

Years ago, chemical dependency was primarily found in poor, urban environments. Today, the drug and alcohol problem is everywhere. In the past, dealers and users hid in the dark recesses of poverty and squalor. Not in the twenty-first century. Today, drugs follow the money, wherever it is found. Alcohol is sold in grocery aisles as well as in liquor stores. Heroin and other drugs are peddled in suburban high schools and in small towns across the country. It is easier to get alcohol and drugs than ever before. And, in my experience, few people understand how to effectively fight this trend.

National and state governments have little to no idea how to handle this epidemic. They shoot conventional policy missiles at the problem, hoping they can eradicate it. But the drug problem today is nuclear. It is so powerful and complicated that governmental efforts seem doomed to failure, while the number of lives lost and families destroyed continues to skyrocket. The war we face and the battles we wage are more than physical. It is also a war for the soul and spirit.

The drug treatment program I run at New Life For Youth deals with the root spiritual issue, using powerful weapons and solutions designed to overcome the inner conflicts that drive addiction. Although the addiction problem is complex and many-faceted, based on more than forty-five years of experience, *I believe that any addict is reachable and curable.* I think of New Life For Youth as the Special Forces in the drug war—God's Navy SEALs of addiction, if you will. We are God's rescue plan, usually called upon to swoop in when all other efforts have been exhausted.

I want you to know that there is hope, no matter how dark, dire, or impossible the situation may seem at this moment. Our God is the God of the impossible, and nothing is too difficult for Him to do. The Bible tells us that Jesus Christ is *"the hope of glory"* (Colossians 1:27). I am living proof of that hope—and so are tens of thousands of New Life For Youth graduates over these many years.

Had someone come to me when I was on the streets, hopeless and totally wasted during my addiction and gang days, and told me that, one day, I would be preaching the gospel and there would be a movie and book about my life called *Victor*, I would have laughed in their face. If they had told me that I would one day start a ministry called New Life For Youth that would help save thousands of addicts, I would have asked what kind of drugs *they* were taking. Now that I've walked this entire journey, I can see the amazing way God has touched lives through the hands of a former gang-banger and heroin addict like me.

After I got clean and began attending Bible college, I felt ill-equipped. I was a high school dropout. Drugs had robbed me of many good things. How could *I* do anything worthwhile?

But one day, I realized that even though drugs had caused so much damage in my life, God was restoring me. He had already healed me, inside and out.

During the Bible school's orientation, the president challenged us with a speech. But my eyes remained focused on a sign behind him. The sign bore a Scripture: *"I can do all things through Christ which strengthens me"* (Philippians 4:13). In that moment, I felt energized with hope and confidence. I remember telling myself, *I can do this with God's help.*

What is God willing to do for your loved one? Anything! All they have to do is submit. But it is going to require a lot of prayer, as well as hard, practical work on your part, before they dare to believe it.

Throughout the years, Isaiah 40 has encouraged me. The Lord sent the prophet Isaiah to Judah because they were about to experience freedom from captivity. To paraphrase the story, the people said, "You're not listening to us anymore, God. You forgot about us. We can't find You. We can't see You anymore."

Sound familiar?

The prophet Isaiah received an answer for them. In essence, God said, "You can't see Me because you've lost your vision for Me. You've forgotten who I am, what I am, and what I'm capable of doing."

Even more impressive was God's further response: "I have forgiven you. And not only have I forgiven you, I have doubled the pardon. All those things you lost in the past, I'm going to give back to you—doubled." (See Isaiah 40:1–2.) Soak this in. God told them that not only had He forgiven them, but He was giving them twice as much as they previously had.

I believe this promise relates to your concerns, as well. How would you like a double blessing?

All is not lost, and it's time to view your loved one's life from a different perspective. Know that God can restore and increase whatever your loved one's addiction has taken from them—and from you!

When I look at my life and consider what God has done for me, I feel like I am the epitome of Joel 2:25: *"And I will restore to you the years that the locust has eaten, the cankerworm, and the caterpillar, and the palmerworm."*

When we surrender our lives to God, the most powerful truth that springs up through the transformation is this: *our past never matches our future.*

We need to know that, as God's children, we have a promise of a better life to come, although we may not see it with the human eye now. Take courage, salvation is on its way; deliverance and healing are coming. Today, there is hope while God works behind the scenes.

My favorite Scripture is 1 Corinthians 2:9: *"But as it is written, Eye has not seen, nor ear heard, neither have entered into the heart of man, the things which God has prepared for them that love Him."*

God did not create your loved one to be an addict or a loser. On the contrary, God created him or her for better things. Although for the moment, it may seem like you are losing your loved one, I want you to know that they have a God-given destiny and purpose.

As Psalm 139:14 assures us, your loved one is *"fearfully and wonderfully made"* by God. He created them for good things, not for drugs or alcohol.

I pray that as you read this book, you receive practical help and spiritual blessing. I want you to know that no matter how bad the picture may look, *there is always hope.* Our God is a Father of compassion, and He understands what it is like to lose a Son and then gain Him back again. You and your loved one matter to God. You matter to me, too.

HOW DO I KNOW IF
MY LOVED ONE HAS A
SUBSTANCE ABUSE PROBLEM?

"Don't panic."
—*Douglas Adams*
Author, *The Hitchhiker's Guide to the Galaxy*

Our cars have all kinds of warning lights. When one of the mechanical systems begins to fail or operate abnormally, a dashboard light comes on.

There are also warnings signs when a person becomes chemically dependent. Medical and psychological experts can pinpoint physical alarms, but most are completely unequipped to recognize the spiritual warnings.

For an addicted person, a spiritual sickness is often the reason they began using drugs in the first place. It's not always because they are depressed, raised in a tough neighborhood, born to the wrong family, or the products of wealth or poverty. Drug addiction is no respecter of a person, culture, or color.

Young people often begin experimenting with chemical substances because they feel they are missing something, but they don't know what it is. They don't understand that God made them for something bigger than the hurting person they are today.

Our God is both spiritual and practical. Therefore, it is important for us to understand all elements of the addiction battle and arm ourselves with every shred of information before waging war. This preparation is crucial for helping those we love and for achieving some peace of mind for ourselves. We must enter this war with our eyes wide open.

DENIAL

Too often, we refuse to see what's right before our eyes. Protect yourself against denial!

When it comes to your loved one, denying or evading the problem of drug or alcohol dependency use can be catastrophic. Awareness is one of your most powerful weapons. At the first sign or suspicion, it's time to act.

Addicts become experts in lying and hiding their addiction. In one scene from *Victor*, the movie about my life of addiction and recovery, my friend is shot by another gang member. For me, that was more than a movie scene. It's a powerful memory from my past. The shooting took place in front of the tenement building where I lived. All the police sirens and street noises drew my mother to our third-floor window. She knew something terrible had taken place. When I walked in the door, my mother asked what happened. She pressed me to reveal whether the commotion was drug-related.

"No, Mom," I lied. "It was over a girl."

She pressed the issue. "Tell me the truth."

I turned to her and said, "You don't want to know the truth!"

She accepted my excuse. At that point, my mother was afraid of the truth, so I got away with a lot of things.

Don't make the same mistake my mother did. It is important that you know the truth of the matter. Never be afraid of it. The truth will set you free in more ways than one. Too many people live in darkness, completely ignorant of the world their loved ones live in—a world of lies, rationalization, and deception. Most kids know how to manipulate and hide their problems. Get smart, and get informed. Love them, but don't believe everything they tell you.

TOO MANY PEOPLE LIVE IN DARKNESS, COMPLETELY IGNORANT OF THE WORLD THEIR LOVED ONES LIVE IN—A WORLD OF LIES, RATIONALIZATION, AND DECEPTION. MOST KIDS KNOW HOW TO MANIPULATE AND HIDE THEIR PROBLEMS. GET SMART, AND GET INFORMED. LOVE THEM, BUT DON'T BELIEVE EVERYTHING THEY TELL YOU.

During the Cold War, Ronald Reagan liked to quote an old Russian proverb: "Trust, but verify." This is still good advice today, especially when interacting with our addicted loved ones.

I'm sure you have a thousand questions. Perhaps you wonder:

+ *What should we do when we suspect our loved one is consuming drugs, or their drinking is out of control?*

+ *How can I know if they are truly addicted?*

+ *What are the first actions to help them?*

+ *What should I do and say?*

+ *What should I not do or say?*

+ *What do I do if they get drunk or take drugs at home?*

+ *How do I rescue my loved one from this scourge?*

DON'T PANIC

Panic is usually the first emotion that grips us when we discover our loved one is addicted. Yet panic-induced fits, pleadings, or rages are the worst things anyone can do upon discovering a loved one's addiction.

When my mom first saw the needle marks in my arm, she suspected a lot of things. In the past, she refused to believe, accept, or even think about my addiction, but the moment she saw those marks, certainty and panic set in. Panicking about the addiction does not make it go away. In fact, it only makes things worse for you and the addict. Rash reactions based on anger or confusion can cause us to make terrible mistakes.

I know people who confronted their loved one harshly and provoked them to anger, which ultimately increased the levels of rebellion. Others coerced their loved ones to make irrational and unrealistic decisions they later regretted. The truth is, you don't want to sever communication, damage your relationship, or drive your loved one away.

In Ephesians 6:4, the Bible teaches, *"And, you fathers, provoke not your children to wrath: but bring them up in the nurture and admonition of the Lord."*

Not panicking is easier said than done. But positive outcomes vastly improve when we step back, exercise wisdom and patience, and refuse to allow fear have its way. Circumstances can blindside us, leaving us helpless to do anything about them. But getting frustrated or panicking does not bring answers nor fix the situation. Fear always turns mice into elephants and mole hills into mountains. When we panic, fear can make us assume the worst. If we don't guard against it, we may torment ourselves with thoughts of doom and gloom, which only make the problem appear worse than it actually is.

If you discover that your loved one is addicted, you need to step back, take a deep breath, then sit down and ask God for help. *"There is no fear in love; but perfect love casts out fear: because fear has torment. He that fears is not made perfect in love"* (1 John 4:18).

Instead of becoming hysterical about your loved one's problem, turn your panic into an asset. Make it work for you. Don't crawl into a hole, but instead, use your anxiety as a stepping stone to positive action. This should be done immediately.

GET SMART

I'm not going to give you a bunch of statistics because I don't think a lot of statistics really help anyone. In fact, they can make you more anxious. But I *will* encourage you to get educated. Unfortunately, in our hurried world, few people take the time to educate themselves about the environment surrounding their addicted loved ones. They suddenly realize they know little beyond surface details about their loved one's friends or where they spend their unaccounted-for time.

Minors are usually more easily monitored, but you must remain diligent. Addicted adults, however, come with their own set of concerns. What can you monitor if your loved one is a spouse, a grown sibling, or a friend with an addiction? Ask yourself these questions:

+ Where do they go before or after work?
+ Do they disappear into the basement or another private place in your home?
+ Are they blowing off family members for "new friends"?
+ Do they have long periods of time when they are MIA?
+ Are large amounts of money missing and unaccounted for?
+ Are prescription drugs disappearing faster than they should?

It is important not to take anything for granted. We live in a fast and evil world in which drug and alcohol abuse are rampant. Because of my ongoing work, I know today's chemical dependency problems make my days of drug use seem more like a visit to Walt Disney World.

If I can pinpoint one big mistake my parents made when I was growing up, it was that they never took time to meet some of my friends. I remember my father's occasional warnings to watch out for my friends, but he did not take time to get to know them himself. He never visited the places where I spent most of my time. He didn't verify what I was really up to. My parents rarely went to my school to check out the environment or talk to my teachers.

In 1 Corinthians 15:33, it says, *"Do not be misled: 'Bad company corrupts good character'"* (NIV). The Bible also says, *"My people are destroyed for lack of knowledge"* (Hosea 4:6).

Don't waste time or energy blaming others for your loved one's addiction. Who knows how the addiction really came about? The truth is, without realizing it, you may have been your loved one's biggest supplier and greatest enabler. I know...*ouch!* But that is in the past!

Besides learning more about your loved one's social circles, educate yourself about the kinds of drugs or alcohol they are using. You may discover some surprising things, and they could be abusing more than one substance.

Here's a hard question: Is your home medicine shelf their supply source?

Many of the medicines legally prescribed today are opioid drugs that deliver the same effects as heroin, and are just as addictive, if not more. Many addicts steal medication from their family and sell the goods to support their habits. They steal jewelry and money. I stole from my mother's purse and my father's wallet. Spouses often clean out savings accounts or safe deposit boxes, in addition to running up credit card balances or opening secret charge accounts.

Some kids deceptively ask their parents to buy them expensive electronic games, then sell them online to get cash. They know if they ask for cash, a parent get suspicious. But if they request a certain game or toy, it's not as obvious. Adult addicts steal and pawn home goods, heirlooms, antiques, collectibles, and other valuable items.

Inform yourself about the possible fabrication or storage of drugs in your house. Check the basement, bedrooms, outbuildings, or other possible hiding areas. Most of the time, addicts become pushers themselves, buying in sufficient quantities to support their own habit on the side. This means they need a hiding place for distribution.

INSTEAD OF BECOMING ANXIOUS AND PANICKING, EDUCATE YOURSELF AND FIND OUT AS MUCH AS YOU CAN ABOUT EVERYTHING CONNECTED TO THE ADDICT: PEOPLE, SUBSTANCES, PLACES, ETC. THIS WILL HELP YOU CREATE AN INFORMED PLAN OF ACTION AND PROVIDE DIRECTION AS YOU REACH OUT TO YOUR LOVED ONE WHILE YOU SEEK HELP AND TREATMENT.

These scenarios may seem overwhelming. Instead of becoming anxious and panicking, educate yourself and find out as much as you can about everything connected to the addict: people, substances, places, etc. This will help you create an informed plan of action and provide direction as you reach out to your loved one while you seek help and treatment.

One of the ways you can protect yourself from paranoia and over-exaggeration is by setting your mind on a truth greater than your loved one's addiction. Keep your strength up by focusing on the promise of potential, not the chaos of the problem.

Do not be anxious about anything, but in every situation, by prayer and petition, with thanksgiving, present your requests to God. And the peace of God, which transcends all understanding, will guard your hearts and your minds in Christ Jesus. (Philippians 4:6–7 NIV)

THE QUESTION OF NARCAN

There is a terrifying new trend among today's young people. They call 911 prior to taking heroin. When paramedics arrive, they often administer Narcan, a medication that blocks the effects of opioids, especially in overdose situations. This can give the addict a false sense of safety and security when approaching the edge of the cliff and cheating death. Too often, the young person loses the game and dies anyway despite the effectiveness of Narcan.

I have reservations about the use of Narcan. I believe it's a modern-day deception. It appears to be an easy escape, like a safe house or miracle second chance for those who overdose, but its saving power is often an illusion.

In my day, we didn't have anything like Narcan. When I overdosed, I was left for dead on a rooftop by my so-called buddies. Before leaving, they turned my pockets inside out and took whatever money I had. I survived because one of those friends felt convicted about leaving me to die and called the police. When officers arrived, they administered oxygen and brought me back to life. I remember waking up and seeing two of them standing in front of me. I got up and tried to run, staggering and swaying left and right. A bitter taste filled my mouth, like I had swallowed something rotten. It was the taste of death. All I could think about was that I had died. But God was not finished with me yet.

Due to the limited medical knowledge of addiction, authorities would use anything to revive those who had overdosed. They would slap you around and shake you. They put ice on your chest and neck. If those methods didn't work, they tried to pour milk down your throat. If all else failed, they gave you shots of salt—not the most pleasant way of revival.

I do believe Narcan may save some lives, but it also provides a deceptive sense of security. I think it sends the wrong message to the addicted world, making them believe they don't have to worry about dying. But if you play the game long enough, you're going to lose. It's like removing the brakes from your car, speeding down a hill, and thinking that if you crash, you won't die. You might get away with it once, but it only takes one failed attempt.

It's amazing to me how we weep for our loved ones, while at the same time, we take away the consequences of their addictions. The sting of danger and responsibility are often necessary wake-up calls.

I believe Narcan is just another way to remove the conviction and fear of death from the equation of addiction. However, it does save lives.

BECOME AN EXPERT IN YOUR LOVED ONE'S ADDICTION

In addition to spiritual strength, you will need mental fortitude and practical applications. You need to become an expert in your loved one's addiction of choice by fast-tracking your education. You are already at a deficit. Start investigating how you can help them defeat this beast.

Find out what kind of drugs your loved one is using, then research their effects and consequences. In America, we are good at making excuses for the enemies of our family and our children. It's as if we have a double standard: we want to save our loved ones from addiction, but we justify the problem by keeping the drugs around.

We do this with many things in our spiritual lives. We sugarcoat wrongdoing and try to ignore the sting of sin and death. But all we do is delay the inevitable. If we want freedom from addiction, it's time to wake up, speak the truth, and smarten up. To reach an addicted loved one, you must learn all the tricks of the ugly substance trade.

Research all the ways chemicals can reach the people you care about. One of the easiest ways is to buy drugs online. I have a friend who discovered his grandson was bringing drugs into the house by ordering them this way. Dealers have found that mail provides an easy delivery and bypasses checkpoints and drug-sniffing dogs at airports and other depots. When chemical substances are smuggled via public transportation, dealers camouflage them by coating them with candle wax or hiding them in other materials to keep dogs from detecting their scent.

If your addicted loved one lives with you, become the greatest detective in your home. Don't take anything for granted. Search their clothing. Empty their pockets. Check their rooms, books, shoes, hats, and backpacks. You have the right because they live under *your* roof. If they are still young and tender, catch them now while they are not so far from your reach.

IF YOUR ADDICTED LOVED ONE LIVES WITH YOU, BECOME THE GREATEST DETECTIVE IN YOUR HOME. SEARCH THEIR CLOTHING. EMPTY THEIR POCKETS. CHECK THEIR ROOMS, BOOKS, SHOES, HATS, AND BACKPACKS. IF THEY ARE STILL YOUNG AND TENDER, CATCH THEM NOW WHILE THEY ARE NOT SO FAR FROM YOUR REACH.

I have a friend who went to prison because his sister turned him in. He was an adult at the time and had been living with her. He bought a safe and told her that it was for the safekeeping of his personal belongings. In truth, he was using it for drugs. She became suspicious when she found a needle and spoon used for cooking heroin. She confronted him and called the police. He ended up serving two-and-a-half years.

Some may think her actions were cruel or harsh. But consider what she prevented. Her brother could have overdosed and died, in her house or somewhere else. She would have lived with regret, wondering if perhaps she could have saved him.

When I found out Tony was in prison, I visited and ministered to him. Once he got past his anger, he realized his sister did the best thing for him. He is now straight, working, and has his own company.

Knowledge brings power; ignorance brings darkness! Sometimes, a true story shows us what words can't.

EMILY'S STORY

I grew up in Richmond, Virginia, the oldest of four children in a loving Christian home. Jesus was so much a part of my early childhood that He was like an extra family member.

My mother took ill after giving birth, and the sickness ultimately pulled our family apart. My parents divorced, which devastated me. I lost everything I had known.

My love for church and God waned behind my anger and disillusionment. By the time I left for college, I was a hard-hearted young woman, determined to live life my way and succeed on my own terms. Even the goals and plans I set for college were replaced with friends, fun, and parties.

I started with party drugs, hallucinogenics, and cocaine. Soon, I found myself wanting more and more. Pills and heroin became more available as my friends changed. What started off as a distraction became an addiction, and heroin became my only drug of choice. My every waking moment was consumed with thoughts of how I would get high that day. I would do anything to avoid being sick from withdrawal.

I lost friend after friend. Some died, others went to jail, and still others wound up in the hospital. After about ten years of deceiving myself, my family, and my friends, insisting I was okay and had everything under control, the bottom fell out. My addiction was open for all to see. I had come to a place in my life where I just wanted to die because I didn't think there was any hope for me.

My mother convinced me to go into a recovery program, although I went kicking and screaming. I couldn't imagine going to a Christian rehab when I felt such ambivalence toward God.

The first thirty days were the hardest. My body screamed with sickness and pain from years of neglect. I felt like I was stuck in a black pit of despair. As I walked around a house full of happy, singing Christians, I couldn't understand what there was to be so happy about.

Little by little, my body started to heal, though I was still spiritually empty. Church was painful as the sermons felt like someone was hitting my rock-hard heart with a hammer and chisel. Without realizing it, I was breaking down.

I eventually stopped resisting and allowed the Word of God to become part of my being. While memorizing a required Bible verse, everything fell into place. I saw my life through a different set of eyes—Jesus's eyes. *"For God has not appointed us to wrath, but to obtain salvation by our Lord Jesus Christ"* (1 Thessalonians 5:9). I understood His love for the first time, and asked Jesus to forgive me and become part of my life. He saved me while sitting on the top bunk bed at New Life For Youth.

The next day, I was a different person. I was happy, at peace, and full of energy. I wanted to learn everything I could about the Bible and Jesus. It was such a drastic change. I don't think the other students around me could have prepared for how different I was. It was not an easy road, to say the least. But I was totally delivered from drugs. Later on in the program, I felt a calling to stay and help other women find freedom and deliverance. Now, every day, I get the privilege of seeing God work in the lives of others and share in His love. Walking in light has been the adventure my heart was always looking for.

When Emily stopped running after the emptiness of the world, God filled her with true satisfaction. Not only did she gain fulfillment as a person, but she also discovered a purpose, a way to contribute to a greater good.

I can only imagine what Emily's mother must have felt during those hard days at the height of her daughter's addiction. In the beginning, she must have questioned whether what she thought she saw was, in fact, real. Were the changes in Emily's habits and behaviors pointing to a bigger problem? Are your loved one's habits a warning light of danger?

If you are concerned and questioning whether what you think you see in your loved one's behavior is real, the following list may help. If you see any of these signs, you are *not* imagining things.

ADDICTION ALARMS

These indications should set off an alarm regarding possible drug use or alcohol addiction:

- Their hygiene habits have become poor.
- Your loved one looks consistently worn down. Their personal appearance is not as good as it used to be. There are dark circles under their eyes and irritation around their nose.
- Your loved one constantly complains about pain or how they are not feeling well.
- They show behavioral changes in arrival times, missed classes, or new routines. Their appetite and sleep patterns have changed.
- They suddenly keep their arms covered up.
- They have a new group of friends and refuse to give details about who they are or what they do.
- They have lost interest in their studies or their job and show signs of irresponsible behavior.
- They exhibit alterations in their habits and tend to isolate themselves. They withdraw from the rest of the family.
- They stay in the bathroom too long or lock the bedroom door.

+ They're incurring extra expenses. They ask for money on a regular basis, or it seems like some of your money is missing.

+ There are new credit card statements coming in the mail.

All of these are potential warning signs of addiction but are often diagnosed as depression. One or more should raise an alarm. We will discuss how to approach your loved one if you suspect addiction has gripped them. It's not enough to know there is a problem—you must also know how to deal with it if you want to reach a resolution.

Learn enough to know the enemy and how it can affect your loved one in the short term as well as for the long haul. This will help you develop a strategy for approaching the problem effectively. Make sure you don't listen to the wrong voices because some people don't have a clue what they are talking about. They may mean well, but they can mislead and guide you into dangerous territory.

As you read this book, I believe your confidence will grow as you are encouraged and provided with resources and tools. I believe you will find hope, even if all seems lost. At the end of each chapter, I provide tips to help you reach your addicted loved one, starting with ways to determine if your loved one has a substance abuse problem.

NEW LIFE SUCCESS STEPS

+ Unless you catch them using, you can never be 100 percent sure whether your loved one is on drugs or abusing alcohol. It is important to find real evidence. Investigate, ask questions, read, and talk to other people. Having clear facts gives you confidence and assurance, and is part of helping your loved one. Remember, he or she is not going to volunteer anything, so dig as much as possible.

+ Think hard about when this all started. What did you see that made you realize something was wrong?

+ Don't ignore disorders and patterns that are not normal, especially when you know something is wrong. The behavior of those with addictions follows patterns that are obvious. It could be anything from the appearance of their eyes to a change in their speech. If the suspicious behavior keeps repeating itself, pay attention. You may be losing your loved one to chemical dependency.

+ Read as much as you can about different drugs and ways to abuse alcohol. Note the symptoms as well as their effects. This will help you to better understand what is happening and where it is coming from. For instance, marijuana is easily obtained in and after school. It can also be accessed at the workplace or when your loved one may be spending time with a friend.

+ Most of the time, substance abuse hides behind the excuse of doing homework, working overtime, or meeting with someone. Do not hesitate to approach explanations with skepticism if the signs align. Better to verify now than to be sorry later. Just don't accuse without evidence.

+ Never confront your loved one unless you have verifiable facts. Don't be intimated by rejection when you try to talk to your loved one. Instead of making accusations or condemning statements, ask questions that allow them the opportunity to come forth and tell you the truth. When this works, you will be in a stronger position to reach out to them.

+ Never hesitate to check their belongings thoroughly. Go into every corner of their closet, look in every pocket, dig into every drawer, and confiscate items you don't recognize as normal.

+ Once you have evidence, lead an encounter with your loved one. Pick the best moment for discussion. You cannot carry on a meaningful conversation with someone who is under the influence of drugs or alcohol, so don't even try. Above all, make your encounter as factual and unemotional as possible. Come from a heart of unconditional love. Keep your speech slow and your tone low. Never approach your loved one with a prosecutor's attitude. Don't dramatize the situation or make this about you by acting like a victim.

+ Stick to the facts. Describe behaviors that have triggered your alarms. Avoid judgment, statements of blame, or insults. Limit yourself to factually describing the misconduct and its consequences. If he or she evades the issue, it's time to press a little harder.

+ Find out how they support their habit and where their money comes from. As much as you can, check all bank account balances and check to see if any objects or jewelry have disappeared from your home.

+ Reinforce your unconditional love with words and actions, but be clear that you will not tolerate their destructive choices.

+ Evaluate the reasons or causes for your loved one reaching the point of addiction. This enables you to tackle the problem more effectively. The reasons may be social or personal, pressure from friends, insecurity, low self-esteem, loneliness, or leisure.

IS ADDICTION A DISEASE OR CAN IT BE OVERCOME BY WILLPOWER?

"We all have the will, but we don't have the power."
—*Victor Torres*

Is addiction a disease or a choice? The answer is, "Yes." Let me explain why both are true.

New Life For Youth, the program I started in Richmond, Virginia, with my wife, Carmen, has taken in young men and women struggling with addiction since 1971. Our proven methods provide a hope and a future for young people struggling with addiction.

Some years back, Lisa, a woman on our staff who overcame her own alcohol and cocaine addiction, had a conversation with a man during a community outreach event. His take on addiction and recovery is one I've heard many times over the years. The man, who appeared to be in his mid-fifties, made it clear he wasn't interested in supporting our program.

"I'm not doing anything to help these druggies," he said.

The look on his face backed up his tone and words.

"I will not give a dime to help them," he added. "These addicts did it to themselves."

He then lit a cigarette and walked away.

When I heard about the man's behavior, I couldn't help but wonder, *If he develops lung cancer from smoking, will he still hold that viewpoint?*

What's your opinion? Do you think he would refuse medical attention since he "did it to himself" with three packs a day since he was thirteen years old? I certainly can't imagine it.

Would he expect his insurance to cover health care costs despite his choosing the activity that led to the condition? I believe he would.

Would you say work-related respiratory issues are a disease or a choice? After all, you could find a different job.

How about joint and circulatory problems brought on by obesity? A disease or a choice?

What's your opinion of an athlete who continually engages in a sport that causes him or her bodily harm? Consider one famous real-life example.

Muhammad Ali was in sixty-one fights before he retired in 1981. According to an interview cited in *People*, Jonathan Eig, author of *Ali: A Life*, wrote about concerns doctors had for the blows the world-class boxer had sustained to his head. According to Eig, "[Ali] kept saying it wasn't going to happen to him, that he wasn't gonna get brain damage."

Ali was famous for wearing down his opponents by allowing them to punch him in the head. A lot. Around two hundred thousand times, according to Eig. Even after the damage became obvious in his slow, soft speech, and he developed tremors, the resolute fighter kept climbing into the ring. But his choices eventually caught up with him. According to physicians who later treated him, Ali was diagnosed with "a cluster of symptoms that resemble Parkinson's disease." His doctors believed the disorder was caused by repeated and frequent blows to the head.[1]

My question about Ali's neurological damage remains: disease or choice?

All of us expect and feel entitled to treatment for whatever medical condition we experience. So why do many people believe that those suffering from addiction don't deserve the same sensitivity and attention?

Conversations with parents, spouses, and children of addicts have revealed that when lives are thrown into such turmoil, we feel better if we have something or someone else to blame. This is why many people fall on the side of addiction as a choice rather than a disease. But they are only half-right.

It is important that we learn to properly diagnose the *causes* of substance abuse, in order to successfully treat the effects. Right now, I'm laying the groundwork for a solid understanding that will ultimately lead to seeing your loved one set free from addiction. I also want you to have a ready answer for well-intentioned family members who may not view addiction in the same way you're learning to view it.

Earlier, I posed a question: is addiction a disease or is it a choice? I answered by saying that it is both. In truth: it is not clearly one or the other. Addiction, like smoking- and eating-related illnesses, is a disease. But it is a disease that begins with a choice.

Some choices people make lead to chemical dependency, and all the consequences that come with it. Since you are reading this book, it's likely your life is being torn apart by those consequences. Your heart is breaking as you helplessly watch someone you love being ravaged by this compulsion. But even in the midst of confusion and pain, I want you to feel encouraged. After all, you're not sitting by and watching it happen. You aren't acting as if there's nothing you can do. You *are* digging in your heels and

---

1. Johnny Dodd, "Boxing Great Muhammad Ali's 'Sad Decline' from Brain Damage Explored in New Biography," *People*, October 13, 2017, https://people.com/sports/muhammad-ali-brain-damage-explored-new-book/ (accessed September 17, 2018).

doing whatever you can to win this battle. You picked up this book. You are turning down the page corners for quick reference because you know there's no time to waste. You've got your highlighter in your hand. You aren't just reading. You are studying for the biggest test of your life. And I'm going to do everything I can to make sure you pass.

As we travel this journey together, some of your beliefs about addiction may be challenged. Please stay open to that possibility, and be willing to adjust your thinking when necessary for the sake of your family—regardless of your reasons for reading.

+ If addiction is completely foreign to you, keep doing what you're doing. Educate yourself. By the time you finish this book, you are going to be an expert in the truth about addiction, even if you've never had a drop of alcohol or touched a drug.

+ Maybe you've struggled with addiction yourself, but you now realize that being an addict and being the parent, sibling, or friend of an addict are completely different things.

+ Or, possibly, you grew up in an addicted household or come from a long line of alcoholics.

Let's talk about this last one. Have you ever heard someone else say, "Addiction runs in my family?" Maybe you've said it yourself. Knowing you have a history of alcoholism or drug addiction can be a warning sign, but it can also be used as an excuse.

The conversation I had with, Karen, the mother of one of our students at the New Life For Youth Men's Ranch is an inspiring example.

She said, "The personality of our whole family is addictive. But you have to make the choice not to act on that addiction. I feel there were certain things I could have done in my life, but I made the choice not to indulge. However, a lot of my family members, including my son, made the choice to indulge."

There it is. Did you notice how she described it? A choice.

I am not a therapist, but I have more than forty-five years of experience working hands-on with addiction. On many occasions, I've spoken with young men and women whose families suffer from generations of substance abuse. Within these families, some members became addicts while others did not. Many of those who did use drugs or alcohol blamed their behavior on their family background. They used genetics as an excuse—a crutch— to give in to the pull of addiction. Others understood that they had freedom of choice and decided not to use drugs or alcohol.

Consider two siblings, children of alcoholics. One becomes an alcoholic and one becomes an accountant. If addiction is inherited, what made the difference? Same heredity. Same environment. Same temptations. Different outcomes. Why? It's simple. They made different choices.

Research has now proven that heredity, in and of itself, does not lock a person into a future of addiction. Possibility does not have to equal probability. Scientific experts have another way of putting it.

The University of Utah's Genetic Science Learning Center published an article about genes and addiction, titled "Susceptibility Does Not Mean Inevitability." I like that. "Susceptibility Does Not Mean Inevitability." It was worth repeating.[2]

JUST BECAUSE YOU ARE GENETICALLY
MORE PRONE TO ADDICTION DOESN'T MEAN
YOU'RE GOING TO BECOME AN ADDICT.
YOU HAVE TO ACTUALLY *TAKE DRUGS* TO
BECOME AN ADDICT. YOU MUST *DRINK ALCOHOL*
TO BECOME AN ALCOHOLIC.

If you have addiction in your family history, this bit of information should give you hope. Yes, you may have some dependency genes—your

2. Genetic Science Learning Center, "Susceptibility Does Not Mean Inevitability," Learn. Genetics. August 30, 2013, https://learn.genetics.utah.edu/content/addiction/genes/ (accessed August 14, 2018).

father might be an alcoholic; your aunt may use drugs—but just because you are genetically more prone to addiction doesn't mean you're going to become an addict. You have to actually *take drugs* to become an addict. You must *drink alcohol* to become an alcoholic.

Our decisions are not passed down like brown eyes and curly hair. Our decisions are not genetic. Our decisions are our own. Still, it's important to be aware of any predisposition toward an illness or disorder.

I'm sure you remember going to a doctor for the first time. You had to show up fifteen minutes early to fill out all the forms. You provided your vital information and your medical history. This background information helps the doctor look for signs of any hereditary issues. If you have heart disease in your family, you may be prescribed low-dose aspirin as a preventative measure, even if you haven't shown symptoms of heart disease. Your doctor wants to get ahead of it. Knowing family history is a great tool in warding off problems.

The same principle applies to addiction. But where addiction differs from hereditary diseases is that the genes aren't the sole deciding factor. Choices are also required. A person cannot become an addict if he or she never uses, regardless of heredity. That door is opened with the key of decision.

You may be quite clear about which side of the choice/disease debate you fall on, but do you know why? Your determination in understanding addiction—how it begins, how it escalates, and how it's treated—is going to go a long way in giving your loved one the support they need to see this through.

MOTIVATION

Let's go deeper by examining what motivates us to answer the disease or choice question. Communication often breaks down in relationships when some family members call addiction a choice and the addict calls it a disease. Is that how it is in your family? Who in your family calls addiction a disease? Who insists it's a choice?

As I said before, when combined, both are right. It's a choice that leads to a disease.

But why do you think some people would rather call it a disease instead of a choice? This is an important distinction because it relates to personal accountability.

Believing addiction is inherited and accepting that it's in a person's general make-up can be a cop-out. Believing substance abuse is a disease for which there is no cure is a motivation destroyer. It lets people off the hook. That belief system takes the responsibility of change out of the hands of the addict and dooms them to remain stuck in their addiction. This is not what we want, and it's not their God-desired destiny.

The good news for you and your loved one, and what brings the addict back to accountability, is that this disease can be reversed if the addict stops using. You can call addiction a disease, but be sure you also use words like *decision*, *choice*, and *goals*. These words empower you and your family to determine the course of the journey, rather than playing helpless victims of some incurable disease. You have a say in the matter. Use the most effective words to point you in the right direction.

YOU CAN CALL ADDICTION A DISEASE, BUT BE SURE YOU ALSO USE WORDS LIKE *DECISION*, *CHOICE*, AND *GOALS*. THESE WORDS EMPOWER YOU AND YOUR FAMILY TO DETERMINE THE COURSE OF THE JOURNEY, RATHER THAN PLAYING HELPLESS VICTIMS OF SOME INCURABLE DISEASE. YOU HAVE A SAY IN THE MATTER.

Accepting the choice to change leads to a cure. Your loved one isn't stuck with the addict life. You are not stuck with this life either. Addiction *is* reversible. It *is* curable.

Curable? Yes, you read that right. *Curable.* Don't start doubting me now. Remember, I'm living proof of that claim. So are thousands of students who have come through our program—like Shelly, who graduated from New Life For Youth's Mercy House.

Shelly says, "Addictive personalities run in my family. When I was doing drugs, I would say it was a disease. That was my crutch. When I started shooting up heroin, it was the most satisfied I'd ever been in my life. But I hadn't met God yet. I didn't have a relationship with Him until I came to New Life For Youth. Now I realize that using was a choice. When you have a disease, it's something you live with forever. But I'm not an addict anymore. I am delivered."

Not an addict anymore. Delivered.

Right now, I want you to close your eyes and picture the addict in your life saying those words: "I'm not an addict anymore. I am delivered."

It's okay if it's hard to imagine. Right now, your life contradicts any indication that freedom is possible. But it is.

Shelly's family couldn't have imagined ever getting past their family history. They came close to just accepting their lot and giving up. But then they did what you're doing now. They got educated. Even when Shelly fought with them, they kept fighting *for* her. It's what you're doing for the one you are trying to save by choosing to find answers and get help.

But you need to know something else. As much attention as we've given to the concept of choice, choice alone doesn't get it done. Choice is just the beginning. If choice isn't combined with follow-through, it's just an idea, not an accomplishment. Choice is where you decide on your direction, but finishing the race takes more than deciding to enter the race. Getting to the end of the race involves many steps. A lot happens between pinning on your race number and crossing the finish line. There are starts and stops. There are stumbles and falls. In this journey from addiction, the power to keep pushing through the pain toward life-long change requires more power than we have. What exactly does it take to live a life of freedom?

People mean well, but to tell an addict they "just need to stop" and that all they need is "a little willpower" is naive. Your husband doesn't want to be an addict. Your daughter did not make addiction her life goal. Telling your friend to "just stop" is insulting. Don't you think they would if they could? Nobody wants to be an addict.

Your loved one is dying, and at some point, no matter what they tell you, they know it. They are hurting and sick and don't want to feel that way anymore. Who wouldn't want to change that life? They just don't have the power to do it on their own.

We all have the will, but we don't have the power.

It's amazing what the will can accomplish. We hear stories of athletes, adventurers, and average people who have done amazing things against all odds. There is a hidden place within people, an inner place that fuels them to go another mile, to hold on another day, and to keep pushing on. Some people call it *self-discipline*; others call it *willpower*.

We've all heard the saying, "Where there's a will, there's a way." The phrase encourages people to give it their all. But what if your *all* isn't enough? What if this addiction is too big for the strongest-willed person to fix?

Even though I used the analogy of a race, recovery is more like a fight for freedom. It's a battle, and not one waged against flesh and blood. Sheer determination isn't going to cut it. This spiritual battle requires a spiritual weapon if you want to win the war.

This is where the Holy Spirit comes in. When Jesus left earth to be with His Father in heaven, He left behind the Holy Spirit as a helper, someone who provides when we need more than our own determination can provide. It sounds like some sort of science fiction story, I know. But this is the truth. I know because I have lived it.

My mother's prayers brought me to Jesus Christ. When I accepted Him as my Savior, I also received the Holy Spirit to help me along the way. This isn't some fairy tale. This is real life. It doesn't matter where you are in your life or what your beliefs are. You might try to argue with my theology, but you can't argue with my experience. I know this works. I did not have the strength to get free from heroin addiction and gang life on my own. I needed the power of this Helper in my life. The results speak for themselves. I have been free from addiction for many decades, and I have seen countless men and women get free from theirs, becoming happy and healthy and whole. Like me, they would tell you it was not through willpower alone.

The Holy Spirit comes alongside us and joins His power with our will-power. He works through our faith and our relationship with God. He works through people and circumstances in our lives. God's support system for us is His Word. According to Psalm 107:20, there is power in it to do exactly what you are trying to do today: *"He sent His word, and healed them, and delivered them from their destructions."*

THERE ARE PRACTICAL CHANGES YOUR
LOVED ONE WILL NEED TO MAKE,
BUT IF THEY WANT THE POWER TO
SEE THIS THROUGH TO THE END, THEY MUST
FIGHT THIS BATTLE WITH GOD ON THEIR SIDE.
WILLPOWER ALONE WON'T GET IT DONE.

There are practical changes your loved one will need to make, but if they want the power to see this through to the end, they must fight this battle with God on their side. Willpower alone won't get it done. To fight this spiritual battle, do as my mother did: arm your family with spiritual weapons.

Please understand, I don't disagree entirely with current scientific theories. I believe science has some facts straight, but I believe it also misses some truth. Science says addiction is genetic and environmental. I agree. It is a disease activated by a choice. But what I've come to know from experience is that a cure is available. Just like the cause, the cure is also activated by a choice—the choice to lay down the chains of bondage and pick up the weapons that will bring an end to this warfare. These mighty weapons can tear down the stronghold of addiction through the power of the Holy Spirit. Let me repeat—*there is a cure.*

David Wilkerson, my mentor and spiritual father, discovered that the Holy Spirit is the foundation of this cure. In his book, *The Cross and the Switchblade,* he wrote, "The Holy Spirit is in charge. As long as He remains in charge, the programs will thrive. The minute we try to do things by our own power we will fail."[3]

Then, referring to the Teen Challenge centers he was opening across the country at the time, David continued: "The Holy Spirit is in charge here. We should write it for all to see on the lintels of every doorway we build. But since that might seem like so many words, we will do better: we will write it in our lives. And in all the lives we can reach out to and touch and inspire with the living Spirit of God."[4]

That truth is just as necessary for your loved one's freedom today as it was in 1962 when David's book was first published. God is still in the business of making the impossible possible.

Are you starting to realize you are not helpless in this situation? You are acquiring knowledge and skills to get your family back on track. You are adjusting your thinking and practicing new strategies. Sometimes it's hard to tell if you're helping your loved one get out of trouble or making it possible for them to get in deeper. We'll discuss the difference between *helping* and *enabling* in the next chapter and walk through the steps to bettering your approach. I want to help you make an impact, and to possibly save and change your loved one's life.

> *For the weapons of our warfare are not carnal, but mighty through God to the pulling down of strong holds.*   (2 Corinthians 10:4)

---

3. David Wilkerson, *The Cross and the Switchblade* (New York: Penguin Putnam, Inc., 1962), 173.
4. Ibid.

NEW LIFE SUCCESS STEPS

+ Watch your language. When you or your loved one are talking about addiction, be sure to use language that holds the addict accountable for where he or she *chooses* to go from here.

+ Heed the warning. If addiction is in your family history, whether it's biological or environmental, be aware of the risk of addiction that comes with certain behaviors. Take a pass on indulging in activities that could result in addiction.

+ Where there's God's way, there's willpower. Freedom is found in Christ. Plain and simple. If you don't have a prayer life, now is a good time to start. If you haven't read your Bible in a while, dust it off. Find Scripture verses that help you fight this battle.

3

HOW CAN I TELL THE DIFFERENCE BETWEEN HELPING AND ENABLING?

"To rescue people from the natural consequences of their behavior is to render them powerless."[5]
—*Dr. Henry Cloud and Dr. John Townsend*

It's hard to know when we're being manipulated. And how do we stop trying to control an addictive situation?

There's a big difference between enabling and helping. Think about it this way. When we enable, we become our loved one's bartender, pusher,

---

5. Dr. Henry Cloud & Dr. John Townsend, *Boundaries: When to Say Yes, How to Say No to Take Control of Your Life* (Grand Rapids, MI: Zondervan, 1992), 43.

or drug lord. It's an easier pattern to fall into than you might think. We can find ourselves trapped in an enabling habit without realizing it. If you discover your loved one has become crafty at using anyone and everyone around them who will buy their stories, then you've become an easy target. Get educated, but don't beat yourself up.

Our most admirable and well-meaning intentions to help can actually make things worse. If it hasn't happened already, at some point, you may realize that your role has been transformed from protector to provider. How does this happen?

As a former addict, I can tell you that alcoholics, junkies, pill-poppers, dopers, and other abusers develop schemes and ways to cheat people like nothing you've ever seen before. They are sneaky and underhanded and they make their rackets so appealing that it's hard to refuse. Becoming a con artist is a natural and nasty part of the addiction process. What happens in the mind of an addict is amazing and terrifying.

Many caring people are easily manipulated due to their own guilt and self-doubt. Others slip into an enabling routine because they are afraid of what might happen if they don't help. And an addicted loved one is only too happy to feed these emotional concerns.

Let me ask you a series of important and thought-provoking questions:

+ Have you found yourself justifying your loved one's wrong choices?
+ Do you pay his or her cell phone bill because at least you'll be able to call them to find out where they are?
+ Do you constantly give them money because you want to help?
+ Do you bail them out of jail or help with attorney's fees because they promised it's time for change and swore that they are ready to go to a rehabilitation facility?

Does this any of this strike your heart and sting your conscience? Month after month, they call you with sob stories of how they had to buy medicine or pay for car repairs, but now they can't pay their electric bill.

"Can you loan me $150 so they don't shut off my power?" they plead.

In the winter, they play on your sympathy. "It's cold outside; I'll freeze."

In the summer, they hit you with, "I'll suffocate without air conditioning."

Naturally, we think, *I can't let them go without lights, heat, or air.* They discreetly push our emotional hot buttons by saying, "You've got to help me!"

Got to? Deep inside, we already wrestle with the question, *Should I?* Then, when our loved one voices the very thing we wonder about, we feel compelled to act on what appears to be a need. That sounds like a rational argument for coming to the rescue. But the real question we should answer is this: *Is my perception being manipulated, causing me to believe an illusion?*

We promised ourselves we wouldn't do it again. We told our loved one the last time would be *the last time.* But how do you turn your back when they could end up on the streets without your help?

We give in to fears that something terrible will happen. He could go to prison. She could end up dead. How can we save them from themselves?

Helping with a small loan seems like the best option available. After all, *how can there be anything wrong with caring?*

Once again, you throw them a lifeline. The trouble is, the lifeline is tied to an anchor. The help you give could actually take them down. By paying their bills, you enable them to keep using their money for drugs or alcohol. You are helping them stay mired in their addiction. You are saving them all right—saving them from facing the tough consequences that could save their lives. All with the best of intentions.

Remember, doing the right thing the wrong way does not make it right.

WALKING IN DARKNESS

When you enable someone, you often do it under the pretense of innocence, under the pretext of love. Bottom line, it is ignorance, and let me be crystal clear—ignorance is the worst darkness!

If you lack information and don't know what you're doing or which way to turn, then you are walking in darkness. Enablers mean well. No one would question their hearts' intent. We want to do the right thing for our families or friends who are in trouble. We don't realize that when we rush in to save the day, we create *hazards* rather than *preventions*. Our protective efforts keep them from finding, or even looking for, the real answers to their problems.

WE WANT TO DO THE RIGHT THING FOR OUR FAMILIES OR FRIENDS WHO ARE IN TROUBLE. WE DON'T REALIZE THAT WHEN WE RUSH IN TO SAVE THE DAY, WE CREATE *HAZARDS* RATHER THAN *PREVENTIONS*. OUR PROTECTIVE EFFORTS KEEP THEM FROM FINDING, OR EVEN LOOKING FOR, THE REAL ANSWERS TO THEIR PROBLEMS.

Creating a Teflon wall around an addicted loved one because you don't want them to get hurt only helps them hide their lies. You end up living the lie with them. You join them in their deadly deception. If you want to see change, you must refuse to rob them of the discomfort that can motivate transformation. Enabling creates an escape from that motivation. Overprotection puts them at greater risk.

If you love an addict, chances are you know how it feels to be manipulated and used. You know what it's like to believe the stories, sacrifice to rescue them, only to discover, once again, that your blind trust and naïve love is helping no one. There is no judgment here. I suspect you feel foolish. But you're not. You are acting out of love coupled with a lack of understanding. You're already doing something about the wisdom deficit by digging into this resource. I want to encourage you to keep the love you feel for them. My story should strengthen your hope.

My mother's love for me didn't keep me from taking advantage of her every chance I got. My love for her didn't stop me, either. That's how strong the influence of addiction is. I loved my mother, but drugs had a death-grip on me.

Be assured, your loved one—whether child, spouse, parent, sibling, or friend—loves you, too. Don't let addiction tell you otherwise. But the things an addict will do to get high defies logic. And the lengths someone will go to save them is immeasurable.

My mother would have done anything for me because she loved me so deeply. At my best, it saved me. At my worst, it made her an easy target. God used her to show me unconditional love and acceptance, but she didn't save me. In reality, her innocent desire to help almost cost me my life.

The last shot of heroin I took was the shot that turned my life around. I didn't pay for it by robbing someone. I didn't steal from my father's wallet to get the cash. My last shot of dope was funded by my mother. Here's the thing—she wasn't trying to get me high; she was trying to get me help. It was a desperate move from a desperate woman.

My own God-fearing, prayer-warrior mother gave me twenty-five dollars to get my fix. She knew that if she didn't provide the money, I would go out on the street to get it any way I could. I would have done my usual: mugged someone, broken into a building or a car, or robbed someone with a zip gun I learned to make in the Roman Lords gang. She knew that's what I would do because I *told* her that's what I would do. My own desperation was focused on manipulating her into handing over the cash. My mother was simply trying to buy me some time.

The night before, I promised her I would go into treatment the next day. But when I woke up, I told her I couldn't because I was strung out and starting to go through withdrawal. Teen Challenge had made it clear they wouldn't take me if I came in high. My mother knew there was no way I would follow through with treatment if I was *dope-sick*, as today's addicts call it. So my mother decided on a dangerous compromise, hoping I would keep my promise. It backfired.

I don't recommend this to anyone. In truth, that last shot could have been the fatal one that took my life in an overdose, or I might have simply disappeared, never to come home again. It was a risk. It was a huge risk.

You might ask yourself, *Why would a mother do that?*

If you examine the situation, you see a woman immersed in panic. She's standing in a room, looking over her skin-and-bones son who is dying. She knows that any minute, the end could come. She doesn't know what else to do.

Maybe you're coming to terms with your own mistakes. If so, that's a good sign. It's much easier to recognize someone else's innocent mistake, especially in hindsight, than it is to see your own unhealthy behavior. It doesn't *feel* good to see where you may have gone wrong, but acknowledging a detrimental pattern is the first step in making necessary changes.

You have to be brave enough to ask yourself the tough questions about how you're navigating through this life and how your choices impact your loved one. What you should be asking yourself is: *What am I doing for/to my addicted loved one that could be keeping them stuck in this addictive cycle?*

USELESS CYCLES OF GUILT AND BLAME

Whatever answer you are willing to identify, know that similar stories are being played out right now, over and over and over again, in families like your own. There is not one parent or spouse I talk to who doesn't desperately want to help their loved one. They are frustrated and don't know what to do. So they keep trying, hoping this time, things will turn out differently. One couple in particular comes to my mind.

WE NEED TO ASK GOD TO GIVE US COMPASSION FOR OUR ADDICTED LOVED ONE. NO ONE IN THEIR RIGHT MIND WOULD CHOOSE TO LIVE A LIFE OF ADDICTION AND ISOLATION. BUT THAT'S THE POINT—THEY ARE NOT IN THEIR RIGHT MIND.

They approached me at church. They had reached a point of exasperation with their son and felt the only solution was to break away from him.

They'd had enough. I noticed the anger on the father's face. I explained to him that he was focusing his anger at the wrong thing. His son was not the enemy. The addiction, the substances controlling his son, were the enemy.

From personal and ministerial experience, we need to ask God to give us compassion for our addicted loved one. No one in their right mind would choose to live a life of addiction and isolation. But that's the point—they are not in their right mind.

I explained to the father, who vented tremendous frustration, that until he recognized his son was being held hostage by addiction, he would be of no use in getting the young man freed. No one blames a kidnapping victim—even if the victim chose to climb in the car with the abductor. Do you see? I'm not trying to take responsibility for their choices off the addict. But as someone who is trying to help them, we have to approach the situation with more compassion and less condemnation. And with more truth.

Part of the addiction cycle causes a person not drinking or drugging to take the most blame on themselves until they learn better. Family members and friends, especially mothers, carry inappropriate shame. The pattern of addiction overwhelms us with guilt for some real or imagined weakness in our relationship, and it drives us to try and make up for it. More often than not, this leads to enabling.

Guilt, defined by Merriam-Webster, is "a feeling of deserving blame especially for imagined offenses or from a sense of inadequacy; a feeling of deserving blame for offenses."[6]

To compound our false sense of guilt, add a lying accuser. When dealing with addiction, keep in mind that we have an invisible enemy: Satan. He will throw mental arrows at us, creating undeserved shame and robbing our families of the life we were meant to have. The Bible tells us in John 10:10: "The thief comes not, but for to steal, and to kill, and to destroy." That is your enemy's mission.

He keeps us so focused on beating ourselves up that we don't have the energy to fight the real enemy. His battleground is in our thoughts. See if you recognize any of these accusations:

6. "Guilt." Merriam-Webster.com, https://www.merriam-webster.com/dictionary/guilt (accessed August 20, 2018).

- *I should have known better.*

- *I'm a failure.*

- *I let my loved one down.*

- *Where was I?*

- *What was I thinking?*

- *Is this my fault?*

- *What will my friends and family say?*

- *Why didn't I catch this in time?*

- *I'm not spiritual enough.*

- *Why didn't I see this coming?*

- *Didn't I pay enough attention?*

- *Did I ignore the truth?*

- *I say I love them, but do I really?*

- *Does God even care?*

Have any of these thoughts crossed your mind? Giving attention to statements like these places the focus on self, making you more prone to mental manipulations. Enabling will never become helping until you stop playing God.

I am reminded of the many times my mother would say, "If I could only get inside of you." She wanted to know how to stop me from what I was doing. She wished she could control both me and the situation.

I replied, "Mom, you can't do anything about this."

She felt helpless. Have your good intentions fallen short or even backfired?

To reach your addicted loved one, you must stop playing God and invite Him into the situation. We need to carry our concerns to God, trust Him to lead us to the right resources, and thank Him in advance for His healing. I understand this may be a difficult concept to see through. Difficult? Yes. Impossible? Absolutely not. *"With God all things are possible"* (Matthew 19:26).

As a parent of four and grandparent of eleven, I understand the instinct to protect and nurture. In marriage, we commit ourselves to our spouses in sickness and in health, for better or worse. With other family members or close friends, we're inclined to offer solutions when we see problems. It's natural to want to act out our care for our loved ones.

Until you reach a point of release, you have no basis from which to work. The idea is to let go of control while still pressing on toward a cure. When you realize you are not giving up on your loved one and accept that you are not the one who can change them, real metamorphosis can occur.

HAVE YOU HEARD THE FREQUENTLY USED SLOGAN OF ALCOHOLICS ANONYMOUS: "LET GO AND LET GOD"? THE *LET GO* PART IS WHAT YOU ARE DOING AS YOU BECOME AWARE OF HOW SPECIFIC BEHAVIORS AND RESPONSES CAN ENABLE YOUR LOVED ONE. RECOGNIZING GOD AS THE TRUE HEART-CHANGER IS THE BEGINNING OF REALLY HELPING.

The Bible is your secret weapon. The characteristics and plan of your invisible enemy are spelled out in the first few verses of John 10. But there's more. Your basis for hope is found in the second half of the chapter. Yes, you have an enemy who wants to take all you have and destroy you in the process. But he doesn't get to decide how this all turns out. John 10:10 says, "I [Jesus] *am come that they might have life, and that they might have it more abundantly.*"

There *is* a good life on the other side of this current darkness. But we have to make room for the One, the only One, who gives life.

God is in the miracle business. Thankfully, that's His job and His business, not yours. Have you heard the frequently used slogan of Alcoholics Anonymous: "Let go and let God"? The *let go* part is what you are doing as you become aware of how specific behaviors and responses can enable your loved one. Recognizing God as the true heart-changer is the beginning of really helping. We become the vessel, the instrument by which God brings a solution to the problem, especially when you get to the root of the issue.

What is at the root? In Andy Stanley's book, *Enemies of the Heart*, he explores each of the destructive forces that affect each of our lives:

+ Guilt

+ Anger

+ Greed

+ Jealousy

These influences infiltrate our lives and damage our relationships. Stanley notes that when left unchallenged, they have the power to destroy our homes, our careers, and our friendships.[7] Which of these heart-wreckers is at the core of your loved one's addiction? Not sure?

In more than forty-five years of ministry, I've seen it proven, time and again. People will tell you who they are if you're paying attention, if you step back long enough to see the true condition of an individual's heart. The Bible says that if you listen, people tell you what is filling their heart.

> *A good man out of the good treasure of his heart brings forth that which is good; and an evil man out of the evil treasure of his heart brings forth that which is evil: for out of the abundance of his heart his mouth speaks.* (Luke 6:45)

Through this lens, you can see how sin has affected your loved one's decisions, and how their lives have become controlled by addiction, whether to drugs, alcohol, gambling, pornography, sex, eating disorders, or any

---

7. Andy Stanley, *Enemies of the Heart: Breaking Free from the Four Emotions That Control You* (Colorado Springs: Multnomah Books, 2006).

other number of vices they may battle. Our addicted family or friends are in the fray. To destroy the enemy, we must identify the weapons used. We need to know how he or she is being attacked.

It's not sufficient to simply recognize her as a drunk or a drug addict. The successful strategy is found in the specifics. Being informed about the particular addiction your loved one struggles with and how they are affected by it will be helpful as you form a plan. Different addictions manifest in different ways.

If substance abuse is the struggle, drug options today are as varied as Baskin-Robbins ice cream flavors. There's a lot of information out there, so be sure you're getting your guidance from a reputable source. For example, a December 2017 article published by the National Institute on Drug Abuse said today's strains of marijuana are different from the ones people used the 1960s and 1970s.[8] Cannabis has been called a gateway drug since the early 1980s. For decades, it has been accused of leading addicts to try harder substances. Today, however, marijuana is much more powerful and itself is considered addictive.

Medicinal marijuana is primarily made from *cannabidiol* (CBD), one of the primary chemicals in the marijuana plant. The reason medicinal marijuana has been referred to as the "hippie's disappointment" is because it is often lacking in THC—the Delta-9-tetrahydrocannabinol that causes the high.[9]

As of June, 2018, the FDA had not approved the full marijuana plant as medicinal but has put its stamp of approval on a couple of the chemicals in the plant in prescription pill form.[10] For our purposes, we're concerned about recreational marijuana and other substances of abuse and addiction. Doing your research will help you to not be deceived by their excuses and your lack of experience and knowledge.

---

8. National Institute on Drug Abuse, "Is marijuana a gateway drug?" Marijuana, June 2018, https://www.drugabuse.gov/publications/research-reports/marijuana/marijuana-gateway-drug (accessed September 17, 2018).
9. For more information on medical marijuana, see https://www.webmd.com/a-to-z-guides/medical-marijuana-faq.
10. See also https://www.drugabuse.gov/publications/drugfacts/marijuana-medicine.

Self-care is another way to protect yourself from enabling. Your loved one's issue didn't start yesterday, and it won't be fixed tomorrow. I'll say this a lot as you read: this is a journey. And you will not position yourself to make it through to completion unless you take care of yourself along the way. Coping with an addicted loved one can consume you. I know you're exhausted. Take time for yourself. Make it happen; no one else is going to do it for you. I know it sounds selfish, but it is not. If your strength is depleted, how will you hold up your loved one and your family?

SELF-CARE IS ANOTHER WAY TO PROTECT YOURSELF FROM ENABLING. YOUR LOVED ONE'S ISSUE DIDN'T START YESTERDAY, AND IT WON'T BE FIXED TOMORROW. THIS IS A JOURNEY. AND YOU WILL NOT POSITION YOURSELF TO MAKE IT THROUGH TO COMPLETION UNLESS YOU TAKE CARE OF YOURSELF ALONG THE WAY.

If you've ever flown in an airplane, you know the flight attendants tell passengers where to find all the lifesaving equipment. In case of an emergency, there are life vests beneath your seat and an oxygen mask drops from the ceiling to help you breathe. They emphasize placing the mask on your face first before trying to assist anyone else—even a child. Having oxygen in place keeps you secure, stable, and breathing. You can't help others if you're gasping for air. Keep breathing and doing what you need to stay strong. Not just for your family, but for yourself.

I know it seems like every moment of every day is all about your loved one's issues and keeping your family's needs met. But you are important, too. You are not forgotten. God wants good things for you. Your health and happiness have to be considered as well.

My mother surrounded herself with people who encouraged and comforted her during my years of heroin addiction and gang life. She had a group of praying ladies who lifted her up so she could continue fighting for my freedom. No enemy could stand against them. Allow yourself to have that type of support.

Surround yourself and your loved one with people who believe in the power of prayer. Then get prayed up! If you don't know anyone, ask God to show you where to find these people.

Your days ahead may be challenging, but through prayer and God's help, you can be victorious over the enemy of addiction. I know from experience, prayer works, so don't be afraid to believe for your loved one's triumph. When I am faced with a challenge, I find myself on my knees. A good little bruise on the knees never hurt anybody. A bruised heart is another story.

YOUR DAYS AHEAD MAY BE CHALLENGING,
BUT THROUGH PRAYER AND GOD'S HELP, YOU
CAN BE VICTORIOUS OVER THE ENEMY OF
ADDICTION. I KNOW FROM EXPERIENCE, PRAYER
WORKS, SO DON'T BE AFRAID TO BELIEVE FOR
YOUR LOVED ONE'S TRIUMPH.

The addiction process brings many moments of heartbreak. You feel it, don't you? The weight of your loved one's condition leaves you barely functioning at times. Feeling that way isn't proof that you're weak or not up for the challenge. It's verification that you're human—and that this is hard. But you will find the strength to keep going if you practice self-care and don't give up hope that your loved one will be delivered.

God is the God of all power. It is His will that you reach your hurting loved one. Cling to the truth-based belief that, through Him, you can help this person. Decide you will not settle for anything less than total victory over the addiction.

I am walking proof that God is still in the resurrection business. I have nothing to brag about except for God's work in my life. Even when I had a needle hanging out of my arm, God knew what was ahead for me, even though no one else, including me, could have imagined it.

To date, my wife, Carmen, and I have traveled to over thirty nations, telling people about God. We founded New Life For Youth and helped an ever-increasing number of hurting young men and women heal. We are founders and pastors of New Life Outreach International, representing forty nationalities. We have satellite churches all over the world. *Victor* is a feature film of my addiction and healing story. I have a beautiful family and a life none of the naysayers would have predicted when I was running the streets of Brooklyn.

I don't share this with you to brag on myself. I offer this as truth-filled hope for your own loved one. God offers a better plan for their life. He sees the amazing opportunities ahead for your loved one, things you can't imagine during this hard season. He sees it because He designed it. He has a personalized plan to give them a better reality, just as He did for me. Let your faith be your fuel.

When you get discouraged and slip back into those old ways of enabling your loved one, let me offer you the scripture my mother held onto when she wrestled her fears. It's from Acts 16:31: *"Believe in the Lord Jesus, and you will be saved—you and your household"* (NIV). My mother kept going back to that promise, even when all signs indicated that I was a hopeless case.

When I dropped out of school and started getting into trouble with the police, my situation appeared to be hopeless. I was arrested three times for drug possession and theft. All the while, my mother may have made some mistakes, but she also did something very right. She enabled me for a time, but also kept going to church and feeding her faith. She refused to give up on me or God. She often preached to me, though I did not want to hear it. She received little support from my father, who was hardened and refused to go to church. He did not want to hear anything about God. He was too busy working and avoiding. Nevertheless, my relentless mother would not be silenced. And though her efforts seemed pointless for a time, she was making a difference. Through my addiction fog, her resolute love echoed across my soul.

Resisting the compulsion to enable your loved one won't be easy. You may feel guilt at first because you aren't helping the way you used to. Remember, enabling isn't helping, it's hurting. Stand strong on God's promise to work on your behalf behind the scenes.

RESISTING THE COMPULSION TO ENABLE YOUR LOVED ONE WON'T BE EASY. YOU MAY FEEL GUILT AT FIRST BECAUSE YOU AREN'T HELPING THE WAY YOU USED TO. REMEMBER, ENABLING ISN'T HELPING, IT'S HURTING.

Don't listen to Satan's lies and don't give up. God has not abandoned your loved one or you. He has designed a future greater than anything you can imagine in this moment. Keep practicing your new way of thinking and responding. Exercise new habits, and though it may hurt at first, if you watch closely, you will see new growth and real transformation take place.

Many people, especially parents, ask themselves what they could have done differently to have kept their loved one from addiction. This is the common emotional trap we will look at next. The quicker we can get rid of the false guilt that drives our own belief and behavior, the quicker we can address the true root of addiction.

NEW LIFE SUCCESS STEPS

+ Honestly deal with your own hurt and pain. We've all had traumas in life. It's imperative we search our hearts and find out how our own issues have lead us to certain behaviors. Has our past indirectly blocked us from effectively handling the misbehavior of our children? Do we give them everything they ask for because we grew up in a poor family? Do we withhold discipline because our parents abused us physically and emotionally?

+ Ask for help. Find a spiritual counselor who can guide you in this process. The right person will help you gain wisdom, spiritual strength, and understanding about how to proceed in this situation.

+ Get support. Look for a support group in your area so you can educate yourself about the unfortunate realities of addiction. Getting a fresh perspective from people who can relate to what you're going through will help keep you strong for the journey.

+ Take yourself out of the victim role. Your loved one does not do drugs or drink excessively to punish you. The more you feel defeated about their addiction, the more difficult it will be for you and your loved one to overcome.

+ Proclaim purpose. Remind your loved one that he or she has a specific purpose in life. Verbalize words of healing and restoration for yourself also.

+ Identify enabling practices. If you recognize your enabling patterns, make a realistic plan to stop these unhealthy habits. Don't let yourself get away with pushing the easy button because you are more comfortable giving in than confronting your loved one with the truth.

+ Don't blame yourself. Practicing tough love and setting up boundaries usually cause guilt and discomfort. Be confident that your loved one needs limits. Face the fact that if you don't stop your enabling practices, he or she may never stop using addictive substances.

IS IT MY FAULT MY LOVED ONE
IS ADDICTED?

"Don't find fault, find a remedy."
— *Henry Ford*

Did I mess up my loved one?"

"Did they inherit this problem from my side of the family?"

These are common questions we hear at New Life For Youth. As we recognize our loved one's addiction, sifting through the myriad emotions we face evokes strong reactions. Trying to find someone or something to blame is a very human, very natural path to follow.

As someone caring for an addicted loved one, you are being forced to live an out-of-control, chaotic life. Labels and liability are the ways in which we try to reduce the chaos to something that feels more manageable. The danger comes when we focus on the wrong culprit and miss the true cause. We can even forfeit the cure when we misdiagnose the problem.

In the last chapter, I explained how to help without becoming an enabler and the importance of acknowledging the true enemy. Remember, your loved one is not the enemy. The enemy is Satan. Even with this understanding, it's natural to sometimes see the addict as the source of all your woes.

After dealing with the consequences of his son's addicted lifestyle for over five years, a father was at his breaking point. The chaos had taken a toll on his marriage and alienated him from his other children. He was on thin ice at his job because of time missed going back and forth to court with his boy. His bank account was dwindling and he was talking about getting a second job. The future looked bleak.

When I met with him, he said, "I'm barely able to keep one job and now I'm looking for another. All to support a kid who's putting his measly paycheck up his nose."

He shook his head, as though he couldn't believe the words he was saying. Then this bearded bear of a man choked back tears of guilt and pain, professing love for his son, while, in the same breath, admitting he didn't like the boy much.

When a parent is pushed to this kind of agonizing confession, it's rough. Who doesn't want to like their own child?

Maybe you have felt the same way. If so, don't beat yourself up over it. This is a reasonable reaction for many parents, caregivers, and others impacted by addiction. What we are really saying is that we don't like what our loved one is doing, the consequences of their choices, and how they are treating you. You've bent over backwards to keep the household together. Now this person, whom you loved more than life, has assaulted you with hateful words.

Not wanting to be around an addict or their messy life is understandable. Human beings go into self-preservation mode when faced with attacks on the family. But you know you can only pull away so much because you do love them and want them to become healthy again.

THE MAJORITY OF ADDICTS WHO COME THROUGH OUR PROGRAM HAVE EXPERIENCED SOME TYPE OF ABUSE IN THEIR HISTORY, WHETHER PHYSICAL OR EMOTIONAL. THESE YOUNG PEOPLE CHOSE DRUGS, ALCOHOL, AND OTHER ADDICTIONS AS A WAY TO ESCAPE THE TRAUMATIC EFFECTS OF THE TORMENT THEY SUFFERED.

The fact is, your desperately lost loved one needs to suck you into their vicious cycle of manipulation. They want you to you to feel trapped, stuck on this seemingly endless hamster wheel of madness.

Recognize the wheel?

You run in circles.

You get mad.

You feel guilty about getting mad.

You get frustrated that you are the one feeling guilty.

You run in circles.

You get mad.

You feel guilty....

Blaming yourself saps your strength as you replay every argument, every minor mistake, as though a few harsh words were responsible for sending your loved one to a drug dealer.

You didn't do that. You are not to blame.

I will speak frankly here. If there have been abuses in the household, if your addicted loved one is a victim of violence or emotional/psychological abuse, that needs to be addressed—honestly and openly.

I know from working closely with the students of New Life For Youth that the majority of addicts who come through our program have experienced some type of abuse in their history, whether physical or emotional. The percentage of those who endured sexual abuse is greater among our female students, but there are men who have endured that torture as well. These young people chose drugs, alcohol, and other addictions as a way to escape the traumatic effects of the torment they suffered.

If this does not apply to you, that's good. I still encourage you to read along with the rest of us. But I cannot gloss over this issue. There are a lot of hurting people who lash out from a place of their own inner torment. Maybe you've heard the statement, "Hurt people hurt people." I'm not sure who originally coined this phrase, but it fits addiction. If you are a hurt person who has hurt others, if the addict you care about was traumatized by your words or actions, now is the time to seek help for yourself. Resolve to get to the root of the issues in your own life.

One of the areas in which our program excels is "whole-family restoration." Whether you were on the giving or receiving end of abuse, we want to see the entire family unit healed and whole. If you perpetrated hurts, there are crucial steps you must take to help in the healing process. I encourage you to speak with a trusted friend, seek counseling, ask loved one for forgiveness, and, most importantly, accept the forgiveness God offers you through the sacrifice of His Son, Jesus.

In 1 John 1:9, God confirms the power of this process: "*If we confess our sins, He is faithful and just to forgive us our sins, and to cleanse us from all unrighteousness.*"

Freedom is available for anyone who wants it. We simply must receive it. And there is strength accessible to us all as we make our way through this life with all its ups and downs and twists and turns. You can keep yourself on track, even when it looks like your whole life is coming off the rails.

Balancing your emotions while your addicted loved one lets his or her feelings run wild is not a job for the faint of heart. Remember, feelings of guilt, as quickly as anything else, will break you down and derail your efforts to help your loved one. It will make you miserable. It will keep you in a constant cycle of blame, dwindling self-esteem, and discouragement. How can you reach anyone else when you allow yourself to sink into a pit of despair and remain there?

Don't feel guilty about your anger. Anger itself is not a sin. It's what you do with anger that can cause a problem for you and your loved one. In fact, anger is a natural stage in the grieving process. And when your loved one is addicted, you can expect to grieve deeply.

We read in Matthew 26:36–46 that, in His humanity, Jesus Himself experienced the devastation of grief in the garden of Gethsemane, where He sweated great drops of blood. In verse 42, Jesus says to God, "O My Father, if this cup may not pass away from Me, except I drink it, Your will be done."

WE NEED TO ACCEPT OUR HUMANITY WHEN
FACING GREAT UPHEAVAL IN OUR LIVES,
ESPECIALLY WHEN OUR EMOTIONS ARE DRIVEN
BY SOMEONE ELSE'S CHOICES.
BUT WE CANNOT ALLOW THOSE EMOTIONS TO
SNUFF OUT OUR DETERMINATION.

Jesus, an innocent man, and God's one and only Son, was facing a brutal crucifixion on a cross. He came to earth as a man, experiencing all of the same emotions and suffering that we do. As a flesh-and-bone human being, Jesus would have preferred to have avoided the excruciating torture of a crucifixion. The *"cup"* He mentions in Matthew 26 refers to the circumstance He was facing. Jesus understands suffering. He is familiar with rejection. He knows, even more than you do, how it feels like to be treated like an enemy when all you've done is love. He was, after all, human.

We need to accept our humanity when facing great upheaval in our lives, especially when our emotions are driven by someone else's choices. But we cannot allow those emotions to snuff out our determination. We must continually fight to find a way out, to be encouraged, and to keep believing there is hope.

As you journey through your own questions, attempting to understand the whys and hows of addiction, be honest with yourself. Sorting through your feelings helps you navigate this natural and normal process. Admitting your true feelings does not mean you are abandoning your loved one, disappointing God, or copping out. The quicker you can rid yourself of unwanted and unwarranted guilt, the faster you can address the real problem, which is the addiction.

It's okay to feel unhappy about the behavior of your loved one and the way they are treating you. I know that, during my days of addiction, I gave my mother plenty of reasons to be upset with me. I can only imagine how she felt when I grabbed her hand, cursed, screamed, and tried to shake her faith by attacking her God. I recall yelling, "You've got to wake up! You are on a trip with this God thing!" But she didn't let my rants stop her. Thankfully, she refused to abandon her hope for me. She kept praying. Not every addict receives this gift. I hope you will give this gift to your loved one.

Too often, our feelings about an addiction situation turn to hurt and result in the rejection of our loved one. The worst thing a person can experience is rejection. The family member or friend of an addict can get frustrated and think it's better not to deal with the problem. So they emotionally check out. They don't realize that shunning someone creates a wall.

When my mom found out I was hooked on drugs, she made an effort to get closer to me. Though she was hurting tremendously, she became even more compassionate and tender with me. Though I didn't show it early on, her consistent love made an impact on me. She always waited up for me into the wee hours of the night. I did not appreciate it then, but as I look back now, I see how her determination kept me connected, even when I tried to pull away.

Sadly, it is not that way in a lot of families and relationships.

In dealing with the spouses, parents, children, and other relatives of the students in our men's and women's homes, you will see many different ways of interacting. For many, communication, confidence, and compassion have become casualties of this war. The breakdown accumulates over weeks, months, and years. But there is an identifiable pattern.

So far, we have discussed how you and your family and friends have been affected by your loved one's actions. No one gets off scot-free. Somewhere along the line, in the soup of frustration and helplessness, each person intimately involved in the addict's life will likely cross a line and respond or behave in a less than ideal way. Raw emotions drive raw reactions.

I understand the commonality of it. The enemy will bring this to your mind, pointing a finger at your misstep as a way to blame you for your loved one's trouble. In your mind, he often taunts, *See what you've done? This is the type of thing that drove him to drugs in the first place. If you were more understanding and patient, she wouldn't be running from you to her addicted boyfriend.*

Be aware of those accusing thoughts. They are lies intended to take down you and your loved one. Take charge of what you allow to enter your head. Those guilt-ridden thoughts pop into the minds of everyone, including me. You're going to make some wrong moves. Don't excuse it but take ownership. As you ask for forgiveness, work to improve, move on, and forgive yourself. We all blow it. But if you repeat these behaviors and leave them unchecked, your slip-ups will become a slippery slope. It's important to consider how others are affected and make adjustments where you can in your reactions. Remember, no one is left unaffected by this situation.

From the perspective of the addict, or even other family members who may feel like they're getting a raw deal in this relationship dynamic, feelings of rejection are common. Spouses or other children in the family have expressed to me that they feel *invisible*. The addict's constant misadventures and mayhem consume everyone's time and energy, and there is nothing left for them.

Maybe you are one of those friends or relatives who consistently put your needs on the back burner because everyone is distracted by another "addict adventure." Maybe you are the one trying to juggle everyone's needs, but there just isn't enough of you to go around. There's no judgment here. This is a messy situation. So many hurting people. So many needs. So many unruly emotions. How do we make the most of every opportunity to reach our lost loved one, while remembering to consider the others vying for our attention? Those people who are waiting in the wings?

When people feel left alone, taken for granted, or not listened to, they can begin to blend into the wallpaper or isolate. When they believe their existence is no longer noticed, they will make subtle turns, until they cease to exist in your life, at least in the way you've known them. Soon, calls aren't returned and the door to their hearts shuts completely. But it doesn't need to end this way.

THE POWER OF RELATIONSHIP

We can avoid losing other relationships in our cloud of emotions if we learn to recognize occasions for acknowledgement. If we don't step through the doors of opportunity God opens, we may miss our chances to reach those loved ones later.

The National Aeronautics and Space Administration understands this concept well. It sends spacecraft beyond earth's atmosphere. But to succeed, the departure and return times must be precise. NASA calls these moments the "open window." If the window is missed for any reason, the mission launch or reentry must be delayed. Otherwise, trouble develops and we miss important moments that keep our other relationships intact.

Maybe your relationship with your loved one has been damaged. You should know that you, as a family member or close friend, have a tremendous advantage. No matter how old they are or how long they have been using, and no matter how they might act or what they might say in response to your concerns, your opinions do matter to them. Your connection is God-given, and no enemy, devil, or addiction can erase the history you have.

One of the most powerful stories in the Bible, is that of the prodigal son found in Luke 15:11–32. Normally, when we hear sermons on the prodigal son, we forget there were two sons. One left the house—he's the boy we've heard the most about.

YOU, AS A FAMILY MEMBER OR CLOSE FRIEND, HAVE A TREMENDOUS ADVANTAGE. YOUR OPINIONS DO MATTER TO THEM. YOUR CONNECTION IS GOD-GIVEN, AND NO ENEMY, DEVIL, OR ADDICTION CAN ERASE THE HISTORY YOU HAVE.

The story of the prodigal son is evidence that keeping the door open makes it easier for them to return. The Bible tells us that once the younger son hit bottom, he came to his senses, realizing that he had made a grievous error. After spending all his money on wild parties and sinful living, he finally realized his mistake when he found himself broke and wishing he could eat the pigs' food.

The desperate young man in the hog slop thought about his father, his home, and the goodness of what he had left behind, exchanging it for all the pain and hurt he now experienced. He had a change of heart and ran back to his father's home. When his father saw him, he was overjoyed and welcomed the son home with open arms. The father planned a celebration and received his son back because he had never given up on him.

But what about the other young man? The responsible one?

While the original prodigal was out running around, the other son was left behind to keep the household running. I imagine he became a little bitter. He may have been just as lost as the son who'd gone missing. He may not have been causing trouble, but I believe he was quite troubled with feelings of resentment, judgment, and disappointment. He let bitterness steal his happiness. Did he feel neglected? Was he starving for attention as his father was distracted with worry for his missing boy? Maybe there's someone in your household who feels that way. Can you relate to the father's dilemma—trying to save one without losing the rest?

Everyone in the addict's circle is affected by their choices. Seeking help for the person caught in addiction is overwhelming. You know that. Attempts at rescuing them can become all-consuming. Maybe your connection to others you care about has been suffering in this whirlwind of addiction emergencies. We'll look more at family dynamics in chapter 10, and address how to help others stay afloat without going under yourself. It is possible. Love never gives up.

It's important to establish and maintain the power of relationship. Strengthen your connection through the bonds of acceptance, encouragement, and unconditional love, no matter how rebellious or bitter your loved one, or other friends and family members, may become in the process. Resolve to make your tie to them unbreakable. This can be difficult, especially where the active addict is concerned.

Your relationship with your loved one is the most powerful deterrent and preventive net you possess. It is important that you build it up and strengthen it as much as you can without ignoring your own needs in the process. Feel what you feel, take your concerns to God, and then get out of His way. Once you release control, the door will open for the addicted one to face their demons. Then God can do His healing work.

You should know that you, as a family member or close friend, have a tremendous advantage. No matter how old they are or how long they have been using, and no matter how they might act or what they might say in response to your concerns, your opinions do matter to them. Your connection is God-given, and no enemy, devil, or addiction can erase the history you have. Family relationships affect us to our core—both positively and negatively, in some cases.

April suffered from feelings of rejection. With no father in sight and her mother addicted to drugs, she found herself alone.

APRIL'S STORY

I lived with my grandparents, and watched my mother come in and out of my life for eight years. It hurt me so badly. I saw other little girls with their moms at school. I wondered, *Why doesn't my mother care about me?*

Even though I knew my grandmother loved me, I questioned how she could let my grandfather sexually abuse me. He was a raging alcoholic and there was no one to protect me from him. I wanted so badly for someone to stop the pain I was experiencing.

When April's abusive grandfather died, when she was eight years old, and the torture ended.

It was as if God finally heard me. My uncle and aunt adopted me and took me to church every week. Even though I was grateful, I longed for that bond with my mother. Whenever she was around, I tried to smile. I hoped a sweet look from me would capture her heart. I hoped she could find a way to love me. But my mom was so caught up in her addiction, she thought being my friend would be better than being my mom.

Since she didn't understand motherhood, she would take me to the bars. Drinking and smoking pot became my life. I was bar-hopping with my mom at the age of ten.

Without the love of a parent, April searched for a sense of belonging anywhere she could find it.

I just wanted someone to hold me and tell me they really loved me. I went from relationship to relationship with men. I would cry myself to sleep, then get up and party the next day. Smoking pot wasn't getting it done. I wanted to escape from my hurt and all the horrible memories of pain in my life. I needed something stronger. So I turned to prescription drugs. I then lost total control of my life and found myself doing anything for the next high. No pill was off limits, and I ended up in jail several times.

Don't get me wrong, I wanted desperately to stop. I even attempted it, but I was all alone and didn't have the strength to do it on my own. Without any support, I found myself back in the lifestyle. Each time I tried to quit, I went back and the addiction was worse than before. By then, I was a mother to three and married. I had a nice home but nothing satisfied me. There was an emptiness in my soul.

Still trying to fill a void in her life, April turned to the hard stuff: heroin.

I was shooting up anything and everything I could find. After stealing a prescription pad from a doctor's office, I found myself in trouble again. I remember one night shooting the meth into my veins, and the rush scared me so badly I saw my life flash before my eyes. I saw my children without a mother. I felt like I was dying.

It was then that I cried out to God, pleading, "Lord, if You get me through this, I will do whatever it takes to get well." I had said that so many times before, I didn't believe it myself. I don't know how I expected God to believe me.

Three days later, my mom ran into some guys who had a table set up outside a Wal-Mart. They were from New Life For Youth's Men's Ranch. My mom got some information about the program and the next week, I applied to enter treatment at the women's Mercy House.

I'm not searching anymore. I surrendered my life to the Lord, and He has set me free from drug addiction and depression. I now know I am loved, as God shows me daily. He has come into my heart and filled me up from the inside out. Today, I am a living testimony that God is our Healer. My family has been restored. I know what it is to experience meaningful relationships. God has completely changed who I am. He has made me who I was meant to be.

I've lived the restored life for several years. Today, I mentor other women like me who are on the journey to freedom.

Sometimes, our loved one's destructive behaviors, including addiction, are ways of self-medicating to try and treat underlying mental or emotional health issues. If you've searched your soul and realize you've played a part in creating those issues, you need to take every step possible to show your remorse and make things right. If you have not played such a part, pray, support, and love them unconditionally, as they strive to cope and heal from their wounds.

But what if you aren't sure about the source of their addiction? Did your loved one turn to substance abuse because of mental or emotional health issues? Or is their behavior the result of their substance abuse? How do you know which came first? Let's explore the need to address underlying issues and causes of addiction next.

NEW LIFE SUCCESS STEPS

+ Check your own behavior without beating yourself up. We always want to do what is best for the people we care about, so taking a personal inventory is never a bad idea. Be willing to make necessary changes without torturing yourself over mistakes and shortcomings.

+ Practice listening. Your loved one has something to tell you. If he or she criticizes or blames you, listen without blurting out defensive answers. Their addiction was their decision, but you want to help where you can. Hearing them out will help you plan your strategy. Listen, but don't validate or tolerate what you know is unhealthy.

+ Show respect. Maintain a calm tone of voice, even if your loved one is not acting respectfully. Communicate from a place of unconditional love, not from a place of shame or failure.

+ Deal with destructive behavior. Confront your loved one with facts and concerns, not fault-finding or compromise. You don't have to sacrifice your beliefs just to avoid a conflict or end an argument. And if they choose to continue their dangerous behavior, remember that you are not responsible for their decisions or responses.

5

WHICH COMES FIRST, DEPRESSION OR ADDICTION?

"You are not what you have done—
you are what you have overcome."
—*Ritu Ghatourey*

On the outside, Tony (not his real name) was attractive, intelligent, and sharply dressed. He fit the stereotype of a young college student with a bright future. However, the more we talked, the lower he hung his head. His smile faded into tears.

I could see his inner pain as he described the shame and hurt he had caused his family. Tony carried an emotional weight that was physically evident, fearing he had lost trust with everyone he loved. The sting of rejection and failure had taken their toll.

Slumped in the chair, shoulders hunched as if an invisible steel beam pressed down on them, his nearly expressionless face told me he had little energy left. When he spoke, his voice was almost a whisper, soft and shaky. When he finally found the strength to tell me his story, I understood why some of the words were stuck in his throat.

TONY'S STORY

I grew up in a good family. We lived on a tree-lined cul-de-sac in a nice neighborhood. Children played in the yards and on Saturdays, dads washed cars and mowed lawns.

My father had a good job and left the house in a suit every morning. Mom worked part-time at the library. We didn't need the money from her job, but she told Dad she wanted to do something productive with her time. She always made sure she was home by the time we kids got off the bus from school. She never failed to have family dinner on the table by 5:30.

Dad and Mom chose this area because it was in a good school district. Education was important to them. I excelled academically and in sports, so from all appearances, they'd set me up for a happy, successful life. Even without all the advantages, the love of my parents should have been enough to make sure I stayed on the right track. Wouldn't you think?

Of course, Tony and his family learned what you and I already know: addiction is not a respecter of persons. It doesn't have a type. Good people who come from good people can become addicts. So where did the well-thought-out plan of Tony's loving mom and dad go off course? What went wrong?

Tony's good grades and athleticism got the attention of college baseball scouts. After looking at the offers and wanting to make his parents proud, he chose the school they hoped he would attend. Classes and ball practice took up a lot of his time, but with his outgoing personality, he also enjoyed an active social life. It wasn't long before his busy schedule included binge-drinking and marijuana on the weekends. Still, Tony was holding it together pretty well—until he wasn't.

His baseball team made it to the championship finals. They had worked long and hard for this and, finally, their moment had come. It looked like they had a real shot to go all the way to the championship. Tony was on the fast-track to go to the major leagues, and this game was his ticket.

Mom and Dad waved to their son as he ran onto the field. It was Tony's time to shine. The sky was overcast, a dream for an outfielder. Tony felt like he was ready for anything. Or he would have been, in any of the other fifty-two games he had played that season. But on that day, as the routine fly ball arced toward the outfield, Tony was high. Off balance, his vision blurred, Tony blinked, stumbled, and dropped the ball. His team lost. The life of professional baseball he'd hoped for, the life his parents had planned and saved for, was destroyed.

The disgraced sports star fell into a deep depression. Memories of that game played over and over in his mind. He heard the boos from the crowd, felt the let-down looks from his teammates and coach, and saw the disappointed looks on his parents' faces. It was too much. From that point on, Tony's life spiraled out of control. To cope with one mistake, Tony opted for a bigger one. He traded up for harder drugs and, as his guilt increased, he sunk deeper and deeper into depression.

Tony's story leads me to a question I often hear: "Which comes first, addiction or depression?"

There are no simple answers, because people aren't simple or the same. Everyone is different. We are different in our neurological make-up. We come from different backgrounds. Tony's story, like ours, has many layers.

When Tony came into our program, his family said he hadn't had issues with depression before. If that's true, from what we see on the outside, the drinking and drugs came before the depression. His dreams were crushed because of partying. If we follow the chain of events, the substances led to a great loss. His response to grief was adding more substances, which drove him to depression. Not all stories unfold in this sequence.

We hoped that once the drugs and alcohol were out of his life, Tony's depression would lift. And that is exactly what happened. Other young men and women who've come through our program with various mood disorders have experienced similar outcomes. Not all, but a great majority find that once they are free of the drug life, they can better handle the effects of their past and envision an incredible future. I'm not a medical professional, but I've learned much about addiction from working with people like Tony. I've also gained knowledge from studying fascinating scientific research.

According to mental health experts, when a person struggles with substance abuse and a mental illness, such as depression, this is known as a dual diagnosis or co-occurring disorder. Researchers at the National Institute on Drug Abuse say that the high prevalence of mental health issues and substance abuse disorders existing together doesn't necessarily mean one caused the other. The article, "Comorbidity: Addiction and Other Mental Illnesses," says, "Drugs of abuse can cause abusers to experience one or more symptoms of another mental illness…. Mental illnesses can lead to drug abuse. Individuals with overt, mild, or even subclinical mental disorders may abuse drugs as a form of self-medication."[11]

Those same experts also report that the treatment of drug use disorders may reduce the risk of developing other mental illnesses. My experience has shown the same. Effectively treat chemical dependency and you can usually improve mental health. That's what we saw in Tony's case.

Over our five decades of involvement with thousands of drug addicts and alcoholics, we have noticed patterns. Typically, if a person tells me they were diagnosed with major depressive disorder when they were fourteen years old and didn't start abusing drugs until years later, chemical dependency was obviously not the cause of their mental illness.

---

11. National Institute on Drug Abuse, "Comorbidity: Addiction and other Mental Illnesses," Research Report Series, NIH publication number 10-5771, December 2008, https://www.drugabuse.gov/sites/default/files/rrcomorbidity.pdf (accessed August 21, 2018).

At other times, someone comes into the program reporting that they started using substances when they were twenty-five. Three years later, after losing everything they owned, they were deeply depressed. In those cases, I am more likely to expect that drugs played a leading role in their mental health issues.

We do not make mental health diagnoses in our programs and would never suggest someone go against what their doctor has told them. But, according to a report from the National Center for Biotechnology Information, "The toxic effects of substances can mimic mental illness in ways that can be difficult to distinguish from mental illness."[12]

Emotional struggles are byproducts of the addiction lifestyle, partly because of how it affects the brain and partly because of how it affects quality of life. If you suspect your loved one may have a mental health problem in addition to their addiction, and their mental health symptoms started long before any signs of substance abuse, you may want to consider seeking a reputable professional. However, if your loved one is in an active addiction cycle, prepare yourself for their unwillingness to participate in therapy.

EMOTIONAL STRUGGLES ARE BYPRODUCTS OF THE ADDICTION LIFESTYLE. IF YOU SUSPECT YOUR LOVED ONE MAY HAVE A MENTAL HEALTH PROBLEM IN ADDITION TO THEIR ADDICTION, AND THEIR MENTAL HEALTH SYMPTOMS STARTED LONG BEFORE ANY SIGNS OF SUBSTANCE ABUSE, YOU MAY WANT TO CONSIDER SEEKING A REPUTABLE PROFESSIONAL.

12. Center for Substance Abuse Treatment, *Substance Abuse Treatment for Persons with Co-Occurring Disorders*, "9 Substance-Induced Disorders," Treatment Improvement Protocol (TIP) Series, No. 42, (Rockville, MD: Substance Abuse and Mental Health Services Administration, 2005), https://www.ncbi.nlm.nih.gov/books/NBK64178/ (accessed August 21, 2018).

Whether depression caused your loved one to self-medicate or your loved one's addiction led to symptoms of depression, you need to hold on to this truth: all aspects of their issues, every consequence of addiction, and each area of pain and weakness have to be addressed, but they can also be healed.

The enemy who sought to devour your family through addiction is the same one who will go after your loved one's mind. The good news: the Word of God will beat him back.

> *The righteous cry, and the LORD hears, and delivers them out of all their troubles. The LORD is near to them that are of a broken heart; and saves such as be of a contrite spirit. Many are the afflictions of the righteous: but the LORD delivers him out of them all.*
>
> (Psalm 34:17–19)

This is a solid promise, no matter what kind of mess you're in or how you got into it.

I didn't get into drugs because I was depressed. I used drugs because I was a thrill-seeker. It was the rush of deception. I believed taking that first fix would make all my problems disappear. I never expected to sink so low or do the things I did in those days. When I put the needle in my arm for the first time, I had no plans beyond my immediate gratification.

If a fish realized a frying pan was the consequence of nibbling the bait, it would never become hooked either. The fish doesn't knowingly choose to be fried up alongside some hush puppies. All the fish wanted was the worm.

This is exactly the way it works with drugs and alcohol. The devil baits the hook and casts out his line to see who will bite. No one takes the first pill or pours the first drink thinking they are going to become hooked. Your addicted loved one didn't mean for all of this to happen. He or she didn't plan for these consequences. They just liked the way their substance of choice made them feel. They liked hanging with their buddies and leaving their cares behind for a while. It was fun. It really was fun.

Until the line tightened and they felt the pull.

Until they were being reeled in a direction they didn't want to go.

The catch is no match for the tension of the hook, the rod, and the reel, unless something or someone comes along and cuts the line. What is that something going to be for your loved one? When will enough be enough? Where is this rock bottom you've heard so much about? It seems like they've hit it a thousand times over. Haven't they hurt enough for one lifetime?

People are led to the door of addiction in search of a thrill or escape from their reality. It's important to see that it often starts with a desire inside the person, but once addiction takes hold, their actual brain function changes. Their distraction becomes their dungeon. The very thoughts and emotions many were trying to cover up with a pleasant high become the four walls of pain, and the addiction trap closes.

+ *Fear* tells us we aren't going to have enough, or we will never *be* enough.

+ *Rejection* proves, in our minds, that our fears are valid. We aren't good enough.

+ *Shame* overwhelms us, telling us that, at our core, we haven't just *done* something wrong; everything about us *is* wrong.

+ *Depression* overtakes us when we lose hope of anything ever changing.

But there is a way up and out of the pit of depression, whether it caused your loved one to turn to substances for relief or was triggered by your loved one's addiction. Different cause, same solution.

Psalm 40:2 tells us that your loved one's rescuer is ready, willing, and able: *"He brought me up also out of a horrible pit, out of the miry clay, and set my feet upon a rock, and established my goings."*

That promise applies to you, too. God will pull you out of your pit of desperation and fear. He will steady you when you feel overwhelmed or defeated. When we experience God as our personal Rescuer and the Lord of our life, we know there is hope. He will see us through. Even if we made wrong choices, even if we saw the hook poking through the bait, even if we ignored all the warning signs, He will still come and rescue us when we call.

Not everyone heeds warnings. For years, cigarettes were promoted as *healthful*. As medical science started connecting the dots between cigarettes and lung cancer or heart disease, many people quit and more avoided the habit altogether. Although legal all over the world, cigarettes are now recognized as a lethal substance.

Not long ago, I visited Costa Rica with my daughter, Rosalinda, and a few of our staff. We participated in a panel of experts on the subject of addiction and recovery. We addressed government officials, university administrators, and volunteers interested in impacting their cities with true and lasting change. Between sessions, we left and stopped at a convenience mart. As we stood in line waiting to purchase our snacks, we noticed the outer packaging of the cigarette packs behind the counter. On the boxes, graphic pictures showed lungs damaged by smoking. They were disgusting and powerful images. In case that message didn't get your attention, there was also a picture of a corpse on the front of the box along with a not-so-subtle message: WARNING: SMOKING MAY LEAD TO A PAINFUL DEATH. With that kind of imagery, you would think cigarette sales would completely dry up.

Even with such stringent warning labels and media campaigns, people still smoke cigarettes. The cigarette companies are forced to produce warning ads, but they still genetically engineer tobacco to contain more addictive nicotine than naturally occurs in the leaves. Manufacturers understand the power of addiction. That power is amplified when mental illness is involved.

The relationship between substance use and mental illness has a long history. The National Bureau of Economic Research reports that people who have been diagnosed with a mental illness consume 69 percent of the nation's alcohol and 84 percent of the nation's cocaine.[13] Becoming knowledgeable about the connection between addiction, depression, and other

---

13. Marie Bussing-Birks, "Mental Illness and Substance Abuse," The National Bureau of Economic Research, http://www.nber.org/digest/apr02/w8699.html (accessed October 17, 2018).

mental illnesses helps us understand the challenges an addict faces, and what we might expect to encounter.

BECOMING KNOWLEDGEABLE ABOUT THE CONNECTION BETWEEN ADDICTION, DEPRESSION, AND OTHER MENTAL ILLNESSES HELPS US UNDERSTAND THE CHALLENGES AN ADDICT FACES, AND WHAT WE MIGHT EXPECT TO ENCOUNTER.

For full comprehension, it's important to review the science. After all, science is man's discovery of what God has always known. But the cure is not found in science, which only lays out the principles. Only God provides the power. Nothing else will satisfy our needs. And that's where addiction starts—with the need to satisfy. There are many things in this life that present themselves as an answer to the void in our heart. But only God can fill our emptiness.

When we were created, God put three components in us: spirit, soul, and body. We have spiritual needs, emotional needs, and physical needs. You can't satisfy physical needs with emotional solutions, nor can you fill your spiritual needs with physical stuff. It just won't work.

When someone begins using drugs or alcohol, they hope to fill the voids in their life. They attempt to satiate their spiritual cravings with natural things. It is a hollow solution. Those who come out of addiction will tell you that recovery is a *spiritual* experience, and that lasting recovery is not about *rehabilitation*; it's about *regeneration*. Even people who slip into addiction through pain medication prescribed for an injury will tell you that something happened to them on a spiritual level as they sunk deeper into reliance on drugs.

Betty (not her real name) was one such empty soul. The poor woman had severe headaches and was prescribed Valium, Xanax, mood stabilizers, and other pain medications. She had been on the drugs for years before realizing she wasn't taking them just for headaches anymore. None of the many recovery programs she tried helped, whether outpatient or inpatient. Her dependence worsened. She resigned herself to the belief that this was her lot in life until she died.

Betty lived with addiction for over twenty years, feeling hopeless to make the necessary changes leading to her freedom. If she had seen a psychiatrist, they likely would have diagnosed her with depression. But she didn't meet with a psychiatrist. Instead, she met with my beautiful prayer powerhouse of a wife, Carmen. Betty described her horrible, seemingly endless cycle of addiction. She wanted out of it so desperately but couldn't find the key.

When Carmen and I sat down with Betty, we shared my story of addiction and how I found release and peace through the love of Jesus. We encouraged her to trust God for her deliverance. Then Carmen and I prayed with her. But that wasn't our only advice. I talk a lot about faith and trusting God, but we aren't meant to turn off our minds and toss away common sense, either. He provides wisdom. It's up to us to apply it to our lives.

We knew it would be dangerous for Betty to quit cold turkey. We advised this sweet lady to work with her doctor to get off the pain medication in a safe way. Her doctor agreed to wean her slowly. Once the drugs were out of her system, she was ready to learn how to live in a new reality. Getting free from the drugs was only the first part of the process. Betty also needed to find out who she was without chemical dependency. She decided to move into our women's home and go through our program. Over time, the spiritual emptiness she had felt was replaced by a realization of her God-designed purpose through a relationship with Jesus. Part of that purpose involved her family.

Like many addicted women who need a whole-life makeover, she faced a bigger challenge. She was married with children, which made her decision to move into a twelve-month residential program even more difficult.

Carmen and I made a commitment to monitor her progress as we ministered to her. We could see the walls of hurt and disappointment come down. She allowed the love of God to reach into her heart and heal her.

After thirty days, this woman's life began to change. The depression lifted. Her family healed. Even her outward appearance brightened as we saw her facial expressions change. By the end of the year, she was a completely different person. She held her head high. It's amazing what happens when we take care of our spiritual life and inner self.

The kind of happiness and restoration Betty and her family found is available for your loved one and family. God's been in this kind of transformation business since biblical times. In Luke 5:17–26, there's a great story of an encounter Jesus had with a man who needed a miracle. Jesus was teaching a group of people, and the Scripture says, "...*the power of the Lord was present to heal them*" (verse 17).

People had heard about the miracles Jesus performed. Word spread that, if you were sick, His presence was the place to be. Multitudes packed in like sardines to hear from him. Everyone wanted to hear Jesus teach, and many prayed for healing.

A paralyzed man was brought to the gathering by his friends. But it was so crowded, they couldn't squeeze his stretcher close enough to see Jesus. They could have given up. They could have said, "We told you it would be crowded today," and then dragged the man back home, promising they'd catch Jesus another time. But they didn't. They were determined to get what they came for on behalf of their friend who could not help himself.

I imagine these friends had carried their friend around for years, catering to his needs, wondering if his condition would ever change. But they never quit. This faithful, long-suffering group of guys lugged their crippled friend up to the roof and lowered him into the room through a hole. He settled right in front of the only One who could make change happen for him.

Can you envision the look on the faces of his friends? Consider what they might have thought. This was the moment when Jesus of Nazareth was going to stretch out his hand and say, "You are healed. Rise up and walk." But Jesus surprised them. He recognized the man's faith, and the faith of his friends. He commended them on it. But instead of speaking physical healing to the man who was clearly paralyzed, Jesus said, *"Man, your sins are forgiven you"* (Luke 5:20).

Wait. What about the healing? What about the obvious physical issue? Medical science would have started treating him for his paralysis before anything else. But Jesus saw the core issue. Jesus saw past the palsy to the priority—the man's spiritual condition. That was the first order of business. The man and his friends did finally hear Jesus say, *"Arise, and take up your couch, and go into your house"* (verse 24). Before Jesus could give the man what he came for, He had to give him what he needed. On that day, the man was forgiven of the wrongs in his life. Then he walked out on his own two feet.

Ultimately, your loved one can do the same.

One day, your loved one will be able to stand on his or her own. In the meantime, make a way to get them in front of the Healer, the Deliverer, Jesus Christ. You are standing at the intersection of your loved one's needs and the One who holds their cure. Addiction is a spiritual illness first, and unless you deal with the source of the problem, you are only placing a bandage on a gaping wound.

By reading this book, you are on your way to saving someone's life. Not sure when to seek outside help? I'll help you make an informed decision in the next chapter.

NEW LIFE SUCCESS STEPS

+ Don't be afraid to ask necessary questions. Do you feel like there's more going on than addiction? Review your loved one's symptoms and the order in which they came.

+ Look closely at their symptoms. Are they having difficulty sleeping? Are they consistently withdrawn? Is there a loss of interest in activities they previously enjoyed? Do they seem to feel worthless or helpless? Are they lashing out in anger? Mental health issues should not be ignored. Seek professional help immediately if you suspect depression.

- Are they making the grade? Younger children and adolescents may fall in academic performance or skip school. Have a conversation with teachers or guidance counselors for a clear view.

- If your loved one seems to suffer from depression, talk to your doctor about co-occurring mental health and addiction issues.

- Initiate conversations about the real issues they are trying to escape. Let them know you love them, you are present, and you are willing to work together to find a solution.

- Talk to them about hope and forgiveness.

6

WHEN IS IT TIME TO SEEK HELP?

"Be strong enough to stand alone, smart enough to know when
you need help, and brave enough to ask for it."
—*Ziad K. Abdelnour*

Could this really be happening to our family? she wondered.

Her husband, Peter, was a good man. He didn't have a college degree, but he was a hard worker and made decent money. He put in long hours for the construction company and drank an occasional beer. But lately, he was becoming forgetful. Somehow, they could never make ends meet financially. He was short with her and sometimes aggressive. There were always excuses—the ones he told her, and the ones she told herself.

He's under a lot of pressure at work.

He doesn't mean it.

She tried to keep the peace and was determined not to argue in front of the kids. Eventually, though, things escalated to the point that she and Peter cursed, yelled, and slammed doors, as their children watched and cried. This was not how she had imagined marriage.

After months of them fighting, the kids didn't cry anymore. Arguing had become their family tradition. Sometimes, the kids joined in the yelling. Everything changed. It became harder to deny the truth of what she saw. She felt like a failure.

Different faces came around as her husband's friends changed. She lied to family and friends when her once attentive and kind husband stopped showing up for family events and school plays. Sometimes, he even forgot to come home entirely. She was scared, so she lied to herself.

The growing pressure began to break her. She asked questions, suspecting what was going on, but afraid to face the truth. She wondered, behind the tears, pain, and anger, *Why does he work all day, stay out all night, and sleep away the rest of his hours? Is Peter using drugs?*

It had crossed her mind before. She was aware of his occasional taste for pot, but he didn't do *serious* drugs. Did he? What was happening to their family?

This is a scenario from one of the families we have reached through our program, but their familiar story could have many names attributed to it. For these people, what started off as small, almost unnoticeable symptoms, ripped their family apart within three months.

When is it time to seek help? If you're asking the question, it's time!

Are you seeing behavior that concern you? It starts with little things. At the beginning of addiction problems, you often miss or justify the small changes that are occurring. You can't put your finger on it, but you know something is up. You may even doubt or second-guess yourself. The pattern is predictable.

At first, you blame it on a bad day. Everybody has them. Your loved one says her sniffles are allergies. The pollen count *has* been up. *Maybe that's the problem*, you think. He sleeps half the day because he couldn't sleep last night due to a dog barking next door. You get a call from school informing you that she was absent twice last week. His boss calls to check on how he is feeling since he called in sick today. He gets quiet and says he has a lot on his mind. Money disappears. Jewelry goes missing. Expensive gear and equipment can't be found. She is fidgety. He flies into a rage over nothing. You've caught them in lie after lie. "Who are these new friends? I've never seen them before," you ask. You are now the one losing sleep and lacking peace.

By this time, your feelings of unrest and concern come more often. It's more than one unusual behavior. The signs get harder and harder to ignore.

Is my kid on drugs?

Is my spouse drinking too much?

Do the kids notice that Mom's acting differently?

Don't try to talk yourself out of these thoughts. Don't try to explain them away. Sometimes, we don't want to hear the truth because we are afraid of what we may learn. But if something is going on that's not right, trust me, it's better to act now than later.

Truth leads to freedom. Denial leads to death.

When is it time to do something and reach out for help? The answer is, it's never too soon, and if they're still alive, it's never too late.

Hope is for the *now*, so it's better to stand up and take that bold step. Ask God to give you the strength and courage to move forward. How many signs do you need if you've already noticed clear changes in his or her appearance, behavior, and moods? If their habits have worried you for a while, there's likely a good reason.

Listen to your intuition. If you know without a doubt that your loved one is doing drugs or drinking too much, reach out for help before it's too late. If you suspect it but think you could be wrong, take assertive steps anyway. If other people have noticed behaviors you try to explain away, seek wise counsel. If you've searched his room or thought about it, find an appropriate counsellor.

It can be difficult and even embarrassing to ask for help when it comes to addictions. But I can tell you firsthand, the difficulty and embarrassment won't compare to the grief of losing your loved one.

IT CAN BE DIFFICULT AND EVEN EMBARRASSING TO ASK FOR HELP WHEN IT COMES TO ADDICTIONS. BUT I CAN TELL YOU FIRSTHAND, THE DIFFICULTY AND EMBARRASSMENT WON'T COMPARE TO THE GRIEF OF LOSING YOUR LOVED ONE.

We currently have a national and global crisis on our hands. You are not alone! Addiction is stealing lives, certainly with opioids, but also with many other types of drugs and alcohol. Families are burying their loved ones way too early. They needed help. Were the signs obvious or hidden? Could any of this have been prevented by seeking help one, five, or ten years earlier? The stories and statistics are staggering.

The hospitals were unprepared for what they experienced that day. "It was like a mass casualty event," the CNN report said when more than twenty-seven people overdosed in a four-hour period. "The calls started coming Monday afternoon, overwhelming the 911 call center and taxing ambulance resources in the area."[14]

This was on August 16, 2016, in Huntington, West Virginia, a community in small town America. More than 440 overdoses had already

---

14. Tony Marco, "West Virginia city has 27 heroin overdoses in 4 hours," CNN.com, August 18, 2016, https://www.cnn.com/2016/08/17/health/west-virginia-city-has-27-heroin-overdoses-in-4-hours/index.html (accessed August 23, 2018).

occurred that year in the rural county.[15] Sad occurrences like this are happening more frequently everywhere.

I'm not trying to scare you, but I want you to know and understand the reality associated with addiction dependency. This scene takes place around the world, from city streets to suburbs to farmlands. This tragedy was more than an evening news report for the people who lived it. Dozens of people experienced devastation when a knock on the door brought the news that their loved one had overdosed. I don't want this to happen to you.

Consider this ABC report from 2017:

"'We have had the highest child removal rate over the last three years,' Brenda Slater, vice president of the Safe Children's Coalition, told ABC News. 'The main issue has been due to the substance abuse…it started out a couple of years ago as pills and we've seen an enormous progression into heroin.'"[16]

This report demonstrates the deep-reaching family impact of a loved one's addiction. The tragic reality is that many children are losing their moms, dads, or both to the trap of drug and alcohol abuse, some permanently, as more kids come home from school to find Mommy or Daddy unconscious on the bathroom floor.

At the Mercy House, the majority of our students are mothers. Most of them young. Most of them single. All of them trying to become who God meant for them to be for their children. We started Mercy Mom's House because we want to give these young moms and their children the best chance at a successful future. It allows women who have graduated from our twelve-month addiction program to live with their kids while they put their newly-learned parenting skills into practice. A lot of emotional healing takes place as these children learn how to trust their parent, while the moms learn to tackle the stresses of motherhood without using addictive substances.

---

15. Tony Marco, "West Virginia city has 27 heroin overdoses in 4 hours," CNN, August 18, 2016, https://www.cnn.com/2016/08/17/health/west-virginia-city-has-27-heroin-overdoses-in-4-hours/index.html (accessed May 31, 2018).

16. Jeesoo Park and Olivia Smith, "Foster parent shortage dire as heroin overdoses rise," ABCNews.com, May 24, 2017, https://abcnews.go.com/US/foster-parent-shortage-dire-heroin-overdoses-rise/story?id=47274193 (accessed August 23, 2018).

In these children, we see the firsthand effects and impact of addiction. Their relationships are affected, their school performance suffers, and their self-esteem takes a hit because drugs came into their lives through a parent who was supposed to take care of them. But healing isn't an impossible concept. The journey has to start somewhere. If we don't bring hope and change to these mothers, what will happen to the next generation? As we've learned, the time to act is *now*. For the sake of your loved one, and everyone else touched by their choices, the time for you to act is *now*, before it really is too late.

I know you love this person, and God loves them, too. Nobody wants to see anything harmful happen to our families and friends who are trapped in addiction.

Listen to what God tells you. What we call *instincts* are often God's whisper, warning and giving us signals. It's imperative that you hear and respond to that persistent voice, telling you what you'd rather ignore. You can't afford to think that this is just a phase that will go away. It's foolish to brush off what you see by labeling it mere "experimentation." I urge you not to take that chance with the life of your loved one.

Recently, I saw something in a young man's face and eyes that spoke to me. I reasoned it couldn't be, not with my expertise and nose for trouble. However, because I was dismissive and failed to pay close attention, things spiraled out of control. Sure enough, I got a phone call informing me that he had overdosed. Lenny was rushed to the emergency room, but doctors couldn't find any drugs in his system. He had overdosed on Benzodiazepine. You may know it by its brand name, Xanax. They couldn't find it in his blood because it was the same medication the doctors administered when he got to the hospital. Thankfully, the overdose wasn't fatal—this time. But so many are.

We tried to reach Lenny, but drugs reached him first. We can never be too careful when it comes to the lives of those we love. I share this as a warning that you can never take things for granted. You cannot afford to take chances. It doesn't matter what substance you suspect holds your loved one hostage, lives will be destroyed or lost if you hesitate.

Don't minimize the risk by comparing the situation to what you may have been involved in at some point. If you've made any of these statements, resolve not to make them again:

"All kids try pot at a young age."

"I experimented and drank at parties with friends when I was in high school."

"I made mistakes, but I turned out okay."

Whatever you do, don't make excuses for the enemy. You've got to come at this thing head-on. Things are not going to work out on their own.

Still not sure? Ask yourself these questions:

+ *What is the worst that could happen if you suspect they're using and you're wrong?* Maybe they get angry temporarily. Maybe you are embarrassed for a moment.

+ *What is the worst-case scenario?* Your loved one gets deeper and deeper into their addiction. They go to prison. Life falls apart. They overdose. And yes, they may even die.

If they *are* abusing drugs or alcohol and you don't seek help, the consequences are life-shattering and tragic. Wouldn't you rather risk embarrassment and your loved one's momentary anger than their life?

So when should you act? The answer is clear. *Now!*

One of the worst regrets in life is wondering whether you would have made a difference if you had only taken action. Far too many people are living with that sorrow.

Be encouraged. It doesn't have to be like that if you act now and reach out in truth and compassion. For those who struggle with guilt for not acting earlier, do not let that hinder you from reaching out today.

I can't give you the exact number of parents who have told me, "I don't want to make him angry" or "I am afraid of what other people will think of me." Let me tell you, no one is going to feel what you feel for your loved one. No pride, guilt, or fear should ever outweigh the love you demonstrate for your loved one. It is better to face the facts and deal with them before it's too late. According to an article by Christopher Jacoby,

Almost everyone has heard horror stories in which someone has lost a loved one as a result of drug abuse. These stories usually involve a series would haves, should haves, if only I had done things differently he/she would still be alive today. Denial is the reason so many addicts remain sick and ultimately wind up dead.[17]

My parents knew what it was like to have your mind forced open by the beast of addiction. It took a while before they caught on to the truth that I was doing drugs. I believe my mother suspected I was on drugs even before she saw the needle marks in my arms. The way I was acting, coming in at all hours, suddenly having wads of cash from drug sales, the weight loss, droopy eyes—they were all dead giveaways. My excuses and lies didn't add up. Still, she didn't want to believe it, didn't want to accept it. But when she saw the track marks, there was no denying the evidence.

At that point, she did something powerful, brave, and gutsy. She didn't try to hide that I was doing heroin. She didn't care what anyone else thought. All she cared about was seeing me delivered. She surrounded herself with positive people, people who fed her faith and determination. She reached out to people who encouraged her. She made me famous by putting me on every prayer list in her neighborhood, as well as those far away. Everyone knew about Victor. My mother had spies everywhere. She went on the warpath, sacrificing all thoughts of herself to save me. I encourage you to do the same.

If you suspect your loved one is using drugs or drinking too much, arm yourself spiritually and practically. Trust God to help. He wants to bring healing to your loved one. Inform yourself about available resources. If you're ready to research treatment options, you might want to flip to chapter 12, "What Should We Look for in a Treatment Program?" There, you'll find ideas for taking the next step.

There's good and bad information out there. People with good intentions may offer you bad advice. It often comes from family members or friends who look in from the outside but aren't experiencing what you are

---

17. Christopher Jacoby, "Denial—The Number One Cause of Death for Drug Addicts," HealthGuidance.com, December 29, 2010, https://www.healthguidance.org/entry/14581/1/denial-the-number-one-cause-of-death-for-drug-addicts.html (accessed August 23, 2018).

dealing with on a daily basis. They likely don't have a background in dealing with chemical dependency. Listen to them but make informed decisions by weighing the advice of others against expert opinion. (See chapter 10 for guidance on how to deal with family.) And don't forget to pray and ask God to guide you to the best options for your situation.

When dealing with addiction, we can become consumed with the emotional drama that often accompanies this lifestyle. Sometimes, we need to step back and evaluate the situation, taking a hard look at the entire picture, investigating every possible fact.

ADDICTION CAN BE AN UNCOMFORTABLE
SUBJECT FOR PEOPLE TO DISCUSS. NOT
EVERYONE AROUND YOU IS GOING TO RESPOND
WITH THE BEST ADVICE. SIFT THROUGH THE
INFORMATION. BE CAREFUL NOT TO SLIP INTO
THE TRAP OF LISTENING TO PEOPLE WHO TELL
YOU WHAT YOU WISH WAS TRUE.

Addiction can be an uncomfortable subject for people to discuss. Not everyone around you is going to respond with the best advice. Sift through the information. Be careful not to slip into the trap of listening to people who tell you what you wish was true.

"They'll grow out of it."

"You're overreacting."

"Give it time and it will pass."

Make sure you're talking with people who have been through what you're dealing with. We need the support of friends, coworkers, and families who have *successfully* dealt with addiction. *Successfully* is the key word in that previous sentence. Those who've walked before you can help you make sense of what's happening because they know firsthand how devastating addiction is. People who have been restored from addiction and thrived are less likely to minimize your situation.

Another resource to consider are addiction documentaries and true-life success stories. Here are a few documentary films to consider. Be warned, however, as some offer raw glimpses into this chaotic world.

+ *The Anonymous People*

+ *My Name is Bill W*

+ *Permanent Midnight*

+ *Victor* (a dramatic retelling of my own story)

Movies can serve as motivation and inspiration. They can help you understand some of the aspects of addiction and offer insights you might otherwise miss, while providing encouragement. In my own story, you will see my decline and rapid transformation into a lifestyle of drug addiction. You may even find yourself in one of the characters as you watch how others deal with my addiction.

Our offices regularly receive emails and calls from people who, for the first time, understand the mindset of their addicted loved one and are hopeful for a new life for their friends and families. Some reach out because they are simply worn out.

Every caregiver gets tired and discouraged, but the Bible provides hope for them, as well as for the addict. If you are trying to take care of an addicted loved one, God is also concerned for you and wants you to be strong. He wants you to feel confident and know that He is with you.

Joshua 1:9 encourages us. *"Be strong and of a good courage; be not afraid, neither be you dismayed: for the* LORD *your God is with you wherever you go."* When you are at a loss as to which way to turn, keep this promise close to your heart: *"Casting all your care upon Him; for He cares for you"* (1 Peter 5:7).

Taking the first step in helping your loved one is not an easy decision. There are a lot of factors to take into consideration:

+ Are you resolved to be fully involved?

+ Is your loved one ready?

+ Have you found the right program?

+ Did you count the financial cost?

+ Do you have a support system in place for yourself?

Let's look at that last point. This is important for you. We all need support from which we can draw strength. You may get help from people like your pastor, others in your church, a close friend, or a family member. But there may also be support groups in your area like Al-Anon and Celebrate Recovery. There, you will find people who get it and will stand with you, helping you through each challenging season.

Strength in numbers is a biblical principle: *"A person standing alone can be attacked and defeated, but two can stand back-to-back and conquer. Three are even better, for a triple-braided cord is not easily broken"* (Ecclesiastes 4:12 NLT).

We all need help, support, and encouragement. There is an element of power and authority when we stand with others in agreement. Pray together, asking God to give you the strength and the wisdom to take on this challenge of seeing your loved one experience lasting freedom from addiction. *"Again I say to you, That if two of you shall agree on earth as touching any thing that they shall ask, it shall be done for them of My Father which is in heaven"* (Matthew 18:19).

Earlier, I asked you to identify your real enemy. I want to remind you that your enemy is not human. It's not your loved one. We fight invisible forces of the spirit world that operate in the minds of our loved ones. These forces work to destroy our loved one's life. This is why our battle plans need to begin with prayer.

As I tell people daily, in order to fight against a nuclear spiritual enemy, we need to fight with commitment, dedication, and radical courage. Have faith in God; put your trust in Him; pray for wisdom and strength. You may have felt abandoned by friends or family who don't understand what you're up against, or why you would commit to helping this addict who has caused you pain. Here is something you can always count on—God is faithful, and He will never leave your side. Deuteronomy 31:6 says, *"Be strong and of a good courage, fear not, nor be afraid of them: for the LORD your God, He it is that does go with you; He will not fail you, nor forsake you."*

Today, after more than forty-five years in addiction ministry, I can report this encouraging news: *the power of prayer still works!* Thousands have testified that when all odds were against them and there seemed to be no light and no hope, God broke through. They are living new lives today. This could be the future testimony for you and your loved one to tell.

TODAY, AFTER MORE THAN FORTY-FIVE YEARS IN ADDICTION MINISTRY, I CAN REPORT THIS ENCOURAGING NEWS: *THE POWER OF PRAYER STILL WORKS!* THOUSANDS HAVE TESTIFIED THAT WHEN ALL ODDS WERE AGAINST THEM AND THERE SEEMED TO BE NO LIGHT AND NO HOPE, GOD BROKE THROUGH.

Many times, when an addict realizes the pain and anguish they have caused others after an arrest or near-death experience, they desire to change. This is what we hope for, but the desire doesn't always last.

Although you may be ready for them to get help, your loved one may not yet have the same train of thought. In the next chapter, we will learn what to do if your loved one refuses help. Their *no* is not always the final answer.

NEW LIFE SUCCESS STEPS

+ Take notes on the differences you've noticed in your loved one's activities; otherwise, you may miss the opportunity to intervene in the early stages. Trust your instincts.

- Make a list of all the facts you can document, then make a list of all your feelings about the addiction situation. Sometimes, looking at our thoughts in black and white can provide clarity.

- If you suspect your loved one is using, ask the hard questions. Don't wait until it's too late.

- Get help for yourself. This will be a tough time. Surround yourself with as much encouragement and support as you can find.

- Get. Help. *Now*. Don't hesitate; don't procrastinate; don't wait until it's too late.

- Pray. Ask the Lord to help you see through all the manipulation and distractions. Ask Him for strength and endurance. Thank Him in advance for the victory.

7

WHAT IF MY LOVED ONE REFUSES TO GET HELP?

"Hope gives you courage when evidence delivers doubt."
—*Lisa Eckman*

I hear it often: "But my loved one doesn't want help."

Perhaps your loved one says nothing at all and walks out, slamming the door behind them as they avoid confrontation. Every time you try to talk to them, it's like discussing things with a brick wall. They shut you down. They shut you out.

We've all heard our share of excuses.

"*Mom, I'm fine.*"

"Honey, you're overreacting."

"I can quit anytime I want."

"I just do it to relax."

"It's no big deal."

Talking to an addicted person who doesn't see his or her need to change is like being in the same room and watching the same television, but seeing different TV shows. How do they not see what you are seeing?

When those excuses, justifications, and flat-out lies come at you, keep an open mind and do not harden your heart. Reaching out to your loved one requires dedication and understanding. Your daughter or son, husband or wife, mother or father, relative or friend refuses to get help because they don't realize how much danger they're in. They are blind. This is a crucial time to pray and ask God to give you understanding and compassion. It's also the time to pray for your loved one's enlightenment, that they would see the truth.

Deep down, they want to be free, even if they don't know it yet. No one in their right mind would choose the life of addiction and all the horrors that go along with it.

In Mark 5:1–20, we find the story of a man who was not in his right mind and hadn't been for a long time. He was controlled by demonic spirits. This guy was so out of control that when people chained him up to keep him from hurting himself and others, he broke the chains with his bare hands. His torment drove him to live in the tombs, where he cried day and night and cut himself with stones. The man found no relief and couldn't get away. He was out of his mind—until the day he met Jesus.

Jesus set him free from the demons that drove him mad. When the people from the region saw the man in his right mind, they were terrified. This is interesting. The people weren't shocked by his naked rants, screams, and superhuman strength. But they were shaken to see him sitting down, wearing clothes, and having a chat with Jesus. Why? Because crazy was the only "normal" they had known from him.

For an addict, crazy becomes their normal. Your loved one will not make sense until the renewing of their mind begins. It seems like a catch-22.

They need to get help so they can have a clear head, but they don't have a clear head, so they can't make the decision to get help.

Don't let this discourage you. As we take this educational journey together, your prayer and preparation will eventually chisel a crack in the lies that keep your loved one trapped in the dark. The light will get through but it's going to take time, as it did for Ricky.

THE STORY OF VICTOR'S BROTHER, RICKY

My brother, a Vietnam veteran, came back from the war with a diagnosis of chronic schizophrenia. As a result of his condition, Ricky lost his family. His wife walked away with his son, never to be seen again. Can you imagine how devastated he felt?

For me, it was hard to know what to do. My efforts included trying to get him into the hospital for treatment, but he responded like I was his enemy.

Change is hard and people will fight it. Someone like Ricky, whose thinking is compromised by chemical imbalance, a disorder, or substances, can become combative and noncompliant to treatment—especially when they've already lost so much.

When Ricky left for Vietnam, he had a bright future. But when he came back, he started drinking and smoking, trying to drown out the horrors of the war. His efforts to self-medicate cost him his marriage, his child, his career, and his home until he had nothing to live for. His drinking got worse. During the height of Ricky's struggles with alcoholism and paranoid schizophrenia, I had a recurring dream. I didn't realize it at the time, but I was being prepared.

Have you ever had one of those dreams where you knew it was more than a fantasy or something you ate the night before? This was that type of dream. The message offered me deep insight. God will do that, you know? He speaks to us, even when we're sleeping. Sometimes, our lives can become so chaotic that it's the only way He can get a word in. And God had something to say to me.

In the dream, I was in the attic of my parents' house in Florida. As I looked through photos and keepsakes in old dusty boxes, two white-gloved hands appeared. The hands weren't connected to anything—no arms, no body. In the dream, a clear explanation entered my mind. *These are the two hands that have Ricky bound and addicted to alcohol and cigarettes.* Even in my sleep, determination took over. I wasn't going to let two disembodied hands destroy my brother! After all, I came from the streets of Brooklyn!

I locked into a wrestling match with the hands. At one point, it seemed as though they were winning the fight, but not for long. I know how to do battle, and I had a powerful weapon. I prayed, asking God to destroy these two hands. Instantly, they lost their grip and faded away.

I understood the dream's purpose. God was confirming the coming breakthrough for my brother. I realize my dream might bring you discomfort, but it's not as far-fetched as you might think. Fighting addiction is all-out warfare. Your mind and thoughts are the places where spiritual battles are fought. On this night, in this battle, I won my Ricky's release through prayer. The daytime reality came a short time later.

My brother sometimes refused to take his medication and then wandered away. On one occasion, he wandered all the way to Puerto Rico! I searched for him in a panic. All I wanted was to bring him home. For thirty days, a full month, we searched for my brother. When I found Ricky, he was living in the streets, drinking heavily, and eating out of a trash can. We did not have a happy reunion. His voice was full of venom when he spoke. He cursed me, saying he wanted nothing to do with me. His words and tone gashed my spirit, but I refused to turn my back on him. Through my dream, God had already revealed the coming victory. I was finally able to get Ricky into a Puerto Rican hospital, where a real miracle took place. Over time, his disorganized thinking became more rational. His volatile outbursts subsided. His mind cleared. He still had struggles, but eventually, I was able to bring him home, where Ricky ultimately turned his life over to Jesus.

After that, I saw a consistent change in Ricky's life. Today, my brother doesn't miss a church service. He is a new man, a veteran who is proud to have served his country with honor.

I often think, *What if I had given up on my brother? What if I had been intimidated and walked away?*

As I've said before, it's easy to slip into a "God role" with our addicted loved one by making the mistake of trying to control their lives. But we are not God. Rather than trying to be God, let's make every effort to be *like* God in the way we love the addict with an everlasting love. God expresses the way He loves in Jeremiah 31:3: *"Yea, I have loved you with an everlasting love: therefore with lovingkindness have I drawn you."*

The Bible shows us the kind of love we should have for others, a love that draws people closer, instead of driving them away. If your loved one is isolating, which is typical of an addict, practice dependable lovingkindness. The *Oxford American Dictionary* defines *lovingkindness* as "tenderness and consideration toward others."

I know. It's easier said than done when they're attacking you every chance they get. But in every situation, we choose how we respond, right? We respond by standing firm *for* them, not *against* them. You may not have had a dream like the one I had, but you are contending with unseen hands holding fast to your loved one. Fight the battle because your consistency will eventually bring the victory, no matter what they say now.

During World War II, London and surrounding areas were pounded by the Germans. Winston Churchill, in a famous graduation speech, encouraged a whole nation. His words still ring true today:

Never give in, never give in, never, never, never, never—in nothing, great or small, large or petty—never give in except to convictions of honor and good sense. Never yield to force; never yield to the apparently overwhelming might of the enemy.[18]

18. Winston Churchill, Speech to Harrow School, October 29, 1941, "Never Give In, Never, Never, Never, 1941," NationalChurchillMuseum.com, https://www.nationalchurchillmuseum.org/never-give-in-never-never-never.html (accessed August 23, 2018).

I believe the key is to not take an addict's angry word as the last word. You've got to understand this. Their *no* is NOT the final answer.

I argued and challenged my mother when she tried to get me to go into a program. I said, "Are you crazy? Stop praying for me. Change isn't for me, Ma. I don't need this. I am all right. I can stop whenever I want to."

But my tiny mother was relentless and she put her trust in God's word, not mine.

You've got to know who to listen to. What is the will of God for people when it comes to salvation? The Bible says that God wants every man to be saved. (See 1 Timothy 2:3–7.) This includes your addicted son or daughter, parent, spouse, extended family member, or friend.

TURNING OUR BACKS ON OUR LOVED ONES OR GIVING THEM ULTIMATUMS IN A PANICKED ATTEMPT TO CONTROL THE SITUATION ISN'T HEALTHY FOR ANYONE AND IT MAY BACKFIRE. I UNDERSTAND WHAT IT'S LIKE TO FEEL SO DESPERATE THAT YOU ARE TEMPTED TO THREATEN AND BRIBE YOUR WAY INTO THE DRIVER'S SEAT OF YOUR LOVED ONE'S LIFE. BUT LOVE DOESN'T FORCE A DESIRED OUTCOME THROUGH ULTIMATUMS.

The person cursing at you and saying there is no need for change isn't looking for help; they're looking for a high. They aren't listening to God. That part is on you. You must listen *for* them, believe *for* them, no matter what justifications they offer to prove they don't have a problem. And remember this—no matter what they say, God gets the last word.

Giving up on your addicted loved one cannot be an option. If or when they walk away from you, resolve to be a constant, steady, determined champion for them. Even when they reject you, make a commitment to stay available when they return?

We decide to be someone our loved one can count on because they cannot count on themselves. When they make decisions that terrify us, how we respond is critical. We have to accept that, as human beings, they have the right to be wrong. And we have to be willing to respect that right. Turning our backs on our loved ones or giving them ultimatums in a panicked attempt to control the situation isn't healthy for anyone and it may backfire. I understand what it's like to feel so desperate that you are tempted to threaten and bribe your way into the driver's seat of your loved one's life. But love doesn't force a desired outcome through ultimatums. We can draw lines and set boundaries, but when they walk away, we never shut the door completely.

Unless you let them, nothing and no one can keep you from caring about your loved one, who is being controlled by addiction—not the drug world, not the devil, not friends, not enemies. Nothing! Your loved one is created in the image of God with a destiny. Their future was never meant to include drugs, alcohol, or any other form of bondage. And no matter what your relationship is to the addict, it is love that will be the catalyst for change.

If you are a parent whose child has your blood running through his or her veins, you have to be strong and courageous. Like Joshua, take a stand for your household: *"As for me and my house, we will serve the LORD"* (Joshua 24:15).

If the addict is your spouse, God has made the two of you one, according to Mark 10:7–8: *"For this cause shall a man leave his father and mother, and cleave to his wife; and they two shall be one flesh: so then they are no more two, but one flesh."*

If you are the child of an addict, you can *"honor your father and mother"* (Exodus 20:12) by staying close to them and showing respect, even though you feel let down.

The Bible says that *"there is a friend that sticks closer than a brother"* (Proverbs 18:24). You can be this kind of faithful friend described in Scripture.

My mother told me, over and over, "Victor, you were not made for drugs."

Your loved one wasn't either. Believe that for them. Don't get stuck listening to their excuses. Any of us can lose hope if we focus on how things appear to be.

The Bible tells us, in James 4:13–14, that we don't know what tomorrow brings. But God does. Our heavenly Father never leaves us. We may turn our backs on Him, but He never gives up on us. Decide right now that you will never, never, ever give up on the possibility of freedom for the one you love.

I know that, right now, it might feel like all is lost. You're looking for a small sign that change is possible, a little flicker of light, but your loved one won't budge.

"No way am I going into some rehab," they say.

Remember, he or she will take a lot of wrong turns before they take the right one.

When the prodigal son took his inheritance, left his father's home, and blew it on wild parties and a wasted life, it seemed as though he had lost everything. (See Luke 15:11–32.) I'm just speculating here, but I bet that the minute that boy stepped foot off his father's property, God already had that pigpen picked out for him. We can't know what our loved one's rock bottom is. But God does. It was in that hog slop that an arrogant young man was humbled and turned back to his family for help.

Addiction is a radical and stubborn problem that has wrapped itself around the heart, soul, and mind of your loved one. But be encouraged— it's not invincible.

Sometimes, a person must fall flat on their back before they can look up. You've got to know that nothing is too hard for God to do. Find people who will agree with you, in Christ's name, and who will believe for your loved one as you do. I am not telling you to deny reality or believe the problem will going to go away without a struggle, but my Bible says, "*If two of you shall agree on earth as touching any thing that they shall ask, it shall be done for them of My Father which is in heaven*" (Matthew 18:19).

Believe that God already has a way to get your loved one to change his *no* into *maybe*. It doesn't always jump immediately to a *yes*.

Sometimes, there's a "maybe I'll look into a program" before they give you that "yes, I'll get help" you've been waiting for. You don't know what tomorrow will bring. You don't know how God is moving and setting things up to get your loved one into a position to ask for help. There may be negative consequences, but those consequences may also save their life and force them to see the reality of their situation.

The addiction race to healing is not a sprint, it's a marathon. We have to be "all in" and prepared to see it all the way through. Freedom is possible, even if your loved one doesn't know it yet. It's during this time that you need to know it for both of you.

God never lets go. NEVER. NEVER. NEVER. He didn't give up on Amanda, as you can hear in her own words.

AMANDA'S STORY

I grew up in a broken home with no father in my life. My mother worked three jobs just to keep us going. When I was twelve years old, I had a cyst on my ear and had to go to the emergency room. The doctor prescribed me pain medicine, and I fell in love.

From then on, I chased that high because it made me feel whole. By the time I was sixteen, I was promiscuous, addicted to cocaine and pain meds, and had tried heroin. Within a year, I was pregnant with twins. Suddenly, I was a single, teenaged, addicted mom.

I was raised with an older brother who was my father figure. He was the only man I had to look up to. My brother taught me how to drive, how to fight my way out of trouble, and how to be respectful. He was my best friend.

In 2009, when I was twenty-two, my life changed forever when my brother passed away. At that point, I stopped caring about living and all my responsibilities. I had done drugs most of my life. But after the worst grief I'd ever known, I began injecting heroin. I just didn't care. I had tried rehabs, spent thousands of dollars, and was more lost than ever.

I had lost sight of purpose and no longer wanted to live. My children were suffering from my lifestyle. Though I really did love them, I just didn't have the power to get off of drugs. I made the decision to sign over my parental rights to a family friend. She adopted my kids when they were about five years old. I haven't seen them since. I had lost my brother, my kids, and decided I had nothing left to live for. I tried to take my own life by swallowing a bottle of muscle relaxants. A few years later, I would try to hang myself with Christmas lights.

After doing some time in jail, I finally got busted on serious charges of fraud and forgery. I spent a year behind bars. I had grown up in church but never understood what a relationship with God was. I found out when another prisoner introduced me to Him, but I wasn't yet ready to change.

I praised God when I was released, then promptly went back to my old ways. My family had given me a job, a home, and all the tools I needed to make it, but I was only interested in forgetting my past. You see, jail is nothing more than a holding facility; it doesn't fix you.

After staying out all night, getting high, brawling, and bleeding, I asked my family for help. They took me to church. That wasn't exactly what I meant.

They had planned it all along, because they knew that Trophies of Grace, the singing group from New Life For Youth's women's home, the Mercy House, was singing at the church that day. My family had this plan that I would willingly go into their program. I was not so willing.

I remember cursing out the director because I was not giving up a year of my life again. I had just gotten out of jail and wasn't about to sacrifice another year. My family played hardball and threatened to call the police. I was high—at the church.

To avoid jail, I agreed to go into the program with every intention of leaving and going back to my old life. I cursed out the house manager, several times. I was livid and scared because I knew I would be very sick with heroin withdrawal. Sure enough, I was, but soon, I adjusted to life at Mercy House. I began asking questions about God. I always had the questions, but was too stubborn to ask. I found myself talking to God, asking and begging Him to take away my pain. I finally surrendered to His will.

That was when I began to flourish. I figured out who I was. I found that I liked myself, which gave me confidence. My whole life was changing. I never thought that inviting God into my life would be the answer to all my problems. When I got to New Life For Youth, I wasn't even convinced there was a God. I never knew He could fix it all.

My life is so different from where it was sixteen years ago. I never thought I would see my thirtieth birthday. Nobody did. When my brother passed away, my mother bought a burial plot for me right next to him. She was sure I'd be next. When our family friends lost their three-year-old daughter and couldn't afford a plot for her, I gave them mine. When I went to her funeral, I walked over to visit my brother's grave. Next to it was this little hole in the ground that was intended for me. In that moment, while I was so saddened for my friend and his devastating loss, I couldn't help but thank God for saving my life. God restored me to the person He always intended me to be.

I work in our church's children's ministry, where I find the greatest joy. The best decision I ever made was giving up a year of my life to let God begin His work in me.

The addiction stories of Amanda and my brother, Ricky, show us what God can do. He wants to give this gift to everyone. If your loved one is refusing help and hope right now, let these stories inspire you to believe that your loved one will be writing one of their own recovery stories one day. Dare to trust that what God did for others, He is willing to do for you. He will always give us what we need to help our loved ones every step of the way, if we turn to Him.

In the next chapter, we're going to take a deeper look at how to stand up for your loved one and stand your ground at the same time through *truth love*. Stubborn love delivers the truth consistently. Truth love will help you win this addiction battle.

NEW LIFE SUCCESS STEPS

+ Don't believe everything you hear. Your loved one may believe that they'll never want help for their issues. You need to believe they will. Believe what God says. God gets the last word. Freedom is possible, even if they don't know it yet. You must know it for both of you.

+ Believe that God has already made a way. Be confident that God is moving and setting things up to get your loved one in a position to ask for help. There may be some negative consequences that come along, but those consequences will end up saving their life, making them face the reality of their situation. The results will be worth it.

+ Dig in. You are the one who can take your loved one into the life God has for them. Be stubborn about being "all in" and see your loved one all the way through.

+ Look deep. Through this process, love can be your greatest motivator to hang in there. Look past the person in front of you to the person they were meant to be. Determine to help them become that person.

+ Continue to get educated and equipped, like you're doing by reading this book.

+ Pray. A lot. Be a die-hard warrior for your loved one's freedom.

8

IS TOUGH LOVE REALLY NECESSARY?

"Building a fence around the cliff prevents a fall."
—*Victor Torres*

Some people are armed and ready to say what's on their mind. Others run the other way at the first sign of confrontation. For many, disagreements are far too uncomfortable. When the one you must confront is an addict, any hope for an honest conversation becomes more complicated.

Do you find yourself reluctant to disagree with your addicted loved one, even on small points, for fear of how they might react? It's common for addicts to become angry and storm off. I've heard it time and again: "If I bring up a problem with my loved one, I will be rejected."

Choosing to back down versus taking the risk could cost you and your loved one much more than a rift over anger. But how do you speak your mind?

Tough love is an expression most of us are familiar with. It means taking a stand for what is true, and saying the hard things.

The definition is simple, yes. But it's easier said than done. Showing tough love is a process. Sharing our concerns and speaking up about what we don't agree with requires courage, sacrifice, and honesty. But the effort is worth it. I would not have known a life of freedom without someone risking tough love for me.

When I was a new Christian and two weeks into my recovery in Teen Challenge, the founder, David Wilkerson, taught me what tough love really was. As part of the program, each student had a chore to do around the house. This was an important aspect of that program, and one we employ today at New Life For Youth. Everyone pitches in. It is both practical and biblical.

Paul says, in 2 Thessalonians 3:10, *"For even when we were with you, this we commanded you, that if any would not work, neither should he eat."* But working and *working with a good attitude* are two very different things.

One of the students was tasked with sweeping off the front porch of the house. He complained about having to do it, thinking he was too good for such a menial job. David Wilkerson, in his direct but loving way, again explained the expectation of the program in terms that left no questions or wiggle room. Several of us were within earshot when Pastor Wilkerson gave the instructions. That wasn't an accident; it was on purpose. Later, Pastor Wilkerson explained what we witnessed was not only for the other young man's benefit, but also for ours. He wanted us to learn the same lesson the reluctant sweeper did. I came away understanding two important messages: first, how to exercise tough love effectively; second, how to build a fence around the cliff to protect anyone else who might wander close enough to fall over the edge.

David Wilkerson didn't miss the opportunity to correct wrong thinking and bad attitudes because he knew a poor work ethic wasn't that young man's only problem. Negativity and the lack of gratitude were his core issues.

David knew that most of us, including myself, had a lot to learn about life. We might have silently agreed with our peer's complaint out of our lack of understanding. But Pastor Wilkerson made sure we all gleaned a valuable life lesson from the experience. He built the fence at the cliff's edge for us.

TRUTH LOVE

Your willingness to tell it like it is may benefit your loved one, as well as others. The truth is life changing when it comes from a place of love. In fact, I have come up with what I think is a more accurate term than *tough love* to describe what we're offering in that important moment.

I call it *truth love.*

Truth love is willing to speak and live out the truth, even when it is hard, even when it's scary and uncomfortable for all involved. David Wilkerson could have let the young man's attitude slide, addressed it later, or ignored it all together. Or, in frustration, he might have flown off the handle. But that wasn't who he was and it wouldn't have been effective. David knew saying the right thing in the wrong way, and not tempered by love, would not have gotten the desired results, especially with an addict.

TRUTH LOVE IS WILLING TO SPEAK AND LIVE OUT THE TRUTH, EVEN WHEN IT IS HARD, EVEN WHEN IT'S SCARY AND UNCOMFORTABLE FOR ALL INVOLVED.

Truth love is not harsh—it isn't selfish. This approach is not about getting something off your chest and it isn't fueled by emotions. Truth love is not impatient, nor does it lash out. Truth without love is tough, but it is not loving.

Truth love is grounded in meekness, but do not mischaracterize it as weakness. The power behind meekness can be compared to a 747 airplane landing. The 747 is a huge, powerful aircraft weighing hundreds of thousands of pounds, capable of traveling over five hundred miles per hour, and carrying over four hundred passengers plus a payload. Though its power is exhibited almost violently during take-off, you see the real exhibition of its strength when it lands.

When approaching the runway, a skilled pilot harnesses the 747's massive power. The four jet-powered engines bring the behemoth onto the runway, where it gently touches down, its strength shrouded in a meek landing.

Truth love controls itself through intentional approaches of meekness, strength, and power. If you get a knot in your stomach at the thought of confronting your loved one, it's understandable. Sacrificing your own comfort for the sake of what your addicted loved one needs shows restrained strength, but it's likely taken you a while to land there.

Trauma resides inside the devastating world of addiction and its consequences. It's normal to feel paralyzed at the thought of approaching your loved one, frightened that something worse could happen. But telling your loved one what they really need to hear, in a firm yet loving way, could hold a cure and prevent worse outcomes.

Truth love acts as a fence, built for the purpose of guarding your loved one against speeding over the edge. Boundaries exist for our protection. Preventive efforts expressed through straightforward, honest communication are not only necessary, but they work.

In my extensive travel over the years, I've had the opportunity to consult with government officials, locally and abroad, and review their addiction response efforts. Organizations are trying, but more needs to be done in educating communities and providing options. The goal is to prevent chemical dependency before it grips and holds.

You might think, *Well, thanks for nothing, Victor. It's a little late for prevention in my house.* But is it?

True, you already have an addicted loved one, or you suspect you do. But it's not too late.

Remember the young man complaining about the broom on the porch of Teen Challenge? He already had a bad attitude. It was too late to prevent his complaints. His wrong thinking spilled out of his mouth. But it wasn't too late for the rest of us who watched the scene unfold.

The truth love David Wilkerson laid on that guy corrected his attitude and prevented others from going down the same path. I realize a bad attitude and your loved one's bad habit seem miles apart in significance, but the principle is the same. The truth, spoken in love, along with a dose of gratitude, can impact both the addiction and the bad habit—and they can affect the people you care about, too.

SETTING AN EXAMPLE

Many of us have other loved ones in our homes who also need guidance and attention. The loved one who is trapped in drug or alcohol addiction may be getting much of the attention, but you must be aware that there are others who are paying attention to you, even if you can't see past the present chaos.

ONE OF THE NATURAL CONSEQUENCES OF ADDICTION IS THE SENSE OF INSIGNIFICANCE FELT BY OTHER PEOPLE IN THE ADDICT'S CIRCLE. MUCH AS WE TRY TO SPREAD OUR ENERGY AND ATTENTION TO ALL WHO NEED IT, ADDICTION IS OVERWHELMING. THE URGENCY OF THE ADDICT'S NEEDS OVERSHADOWS EVERYTHING AND EVERYONE ELSE.

One of the natural consequences of addiction is the sense of insignificance felt by other people in the addict's circle. Much as we try to spread our energy and attention to all who need it, addiction is overwhelming. The urgency of the addict's needs overshadows everything and everyone else. Awareness can help us combat peripheral fallout.

Compassionately verbalizing the hard truth of the situation to everyone touched by addiction provides a safe environment for all. Truth love will protect or create a healthy and sober environment for everyone involved. You are far better equipped to do that now than you once were.

Most people who have experienced life with an addicted loved one can say, "If I only knew then what I know now!" We can't go back in time, but we can move forward using what we know now. As caregivers, if we open our eyes and become aware of all those who are watching from the sidelines, we may be able to keep our *other* loved ones from falling into the grips of addiction by not hiding or denying the truth.

In the early days of New Life For Youth, my four children grew up at our program's New Life Ranch. We had an apartment on-site, and though it wasn't huge, you would be amazed at how many people we could get in there, especially at mealtime.

It was rarely just our family of six sitting around the kitchen table. When Carmen started cooking, the guys in the program would make their way into our little home. With students in all stages of recovery, you can imagine the eye-opening, jaw-dropping conversations that took place over dinner. I could have shielded my kids by insisting that they remain isolated from the chaos. Instead, I used this opportunity to educate them and build a preventive fence in their lives.

Today, our three daughters and son are all considered experts in addiction, though they have never been addicts or received formal education on the subject. But because they were in earshot of the lessons being taught to men and women with a history of substance abuse, they learned that they did not want any part of that life.

Do you see what happened? Whether it's other family members, friends, your addicted loved one's friends, or complete strangers, people are watching how you handle this. Truth love not only helps the addict but it can also prevent others from entering the dark world of chemical dependency. Honesty provides a fence of safety. But for full effectiveness, we had better know *where* we stand.

CHECK YOURSELF

We all should stop and do a little soul-searching. We need to consider our own condition. We need to investigate ourselves before we can initiate change in others. There's no room for the error of double standard. Hypocrisy is the enemy of influence.

We are all human. Perfection isn't required in order to guide someone. But turning a little truth love on yourself and taking your own advice is. We need to remain firm, fair, and consistent so our loved one hears us *and* is receptive to our input. The book of James speaks of heeding instruction, not just hearing it. *"But be you doers of the word, and not hearers only, deceiving your own selves"* (James 1:22).

As you meditate on this Bible verse, consider the following:

- What is my relationship with substances such as tobacco, alcohol, or prescription and non-prescription drugs?
- Do I have secret sins, things I would ashamed of anyone knowing?
- Do the things I do for entertainment strengthen my mind in healthy ways?
- Who are the people of influence in my life?
- Who am I accountable to?

After we assess the foundation of our own lives, we can work to reshape the environments we are responsible for. Before we can *speak* the truth, we have to *know* the truth. We might have to challenge what we believe about things we have accepted as normal. We might have to admit that we are affected by that which we surrounded ourselves.

I won't go on a tangent, but we need to be careful about the things we allow to enter our minds. Are you familiar with this children's song from Sunday school?

O, be careful little eyes what you see.

O, be careful little eyes what you see.

There's a Father up above

And He's looking down in love.

So, be careful little eyes what you see.[19]

This is a song about prevention. It also warns us to guard our ears, hands, feet, and mouths—every gateway through which the enemy enters our lives. Regardless of what society chooses, we must not be careless.

I'm giving you a heavy dose of truth love right now. I want to see you, your family, and your friends become everything you were meant to be. But that won't happen unless you value yourself and your environment—theirs, too.

Preventions are practical. Many of us have car alarms because we want to protect them from being stolen. We have gated communities, requiring a code to enter. Our homes have little signs in the yard, announcing to thieves that we have security systems. We batten down our windows, latch our doors, and put locks on our bicycles. We have safety deposit boxes that require not one, but two keys. Some art museums have laser beams and motion sensors. Preventative measures keep our things safe. We go to great lengths to protect what's ours.

Everything I've mentioned is stuff. It might be expensive stuff, but it's still just stuff. If we placed that kind of value on the condition of the people around us, we would set up more roadblocks and warnings to protect them. We don't have the luxury of wavering or backing down with addiction. Your loved one's life is at risk. How does the risk of them being upset with you compare to that? So, step up—and, when appropriate, step back.

TRUTH AND CONSEQUENCES

Another way to exhibit truth love is allowing your loved one to experience the consequences of their actions through the school of hard knocks. For most of us, not jumping in to rescue them is excruciating. Even though

---

19. "O Be Careful Little Eyes What You See," (Zondervan Music Publishers, 1956).

it may be within our means, it may not always be in the best interest of our loved one to provide an escape. That's the difference between *enabling* and *helping* them, which we discussed in the third chapter.

I once offered support to a doctor whose daughter was addicted to heroin. He had tried everything to reach her but without success. Eventually, she landed in jail. Knowing her father had the money, she called him to bail her out. The dad couldn't stand the thought of his child being behind bars. Not knowing what to do, he called me.

I told him, bluntly, "Leave her in jail."

He questioned my answer. "What kind of dad would I be if I left her there when she knows I'm perfectly able to bail her out?"

"The kind of father who loves his child enough to let her be angry at him in order to save her life."

YOU DON'T HAVE TO HAVE ALL THE ANSWERS.
YOU JUST HAVE TO BE WILLING TO FIND THEM.
WISE COUNSEL AND PRAYER, ALONG WITH THE
GUIDANCE AND STRENGTH FOUND IN THE BIBLE,
CAN PROVIDE THE DIRECTION YOU NEED.

When our loved one experiences consequences, it could save them from more devastating outcomes later. This father took my advice. He let her stay in jail, then made arrangements for her to enter the New Life For Youth women's program when she was released. She initially had her ups and downs, but once she surrendered, she got the deliverance she needed to graduate and go on to live a healthy life. Today, she is a married woman with four children. She and her husband own a prosperous business together. But what would have happened if her father had paid the bail and she walked out, free and easy? She would have gone right back to drug use after being clean for thirty days. She could have overdosed, and he would have lost her forever.

The truth love that doctor used with his daughter was based on the counsel of someone he trusted who knew about addiction. If you encounter a situation and aren't sure if you should step up or step back, do what this man did and contact someone with experience who can guide you. You don't have to have all the answers. You just have to be willing to find them. Wise counsel and prayer, along with the guidance and strength found in the Bible, can provide the direction you need.

Truth love is genuine love. It's the love of Jesus, the love of God. We can find direction and courage in that love. But we need to be a straight shooter, not beat around the bush or give in to things we know aren't best for our loved one. We want to see them set free. There's no freedom in compromise. The truth is spoken, even if it's hard to hear.

I remember a New Life Ranch student who came to me one day and said, "You know, I've been in this program three months. I'm changed, yet my wife won't forgive me and accept me back."

I asked him, "How long were you a drug addict?"

He said, "About twelve years."

I smiled, put my hand on his shoulder, and said, "You were a drug addict for twelve years, and you want your wife to believe in you after ninety days of sobriety? You've got to be kidding me."

This young man didn't have the slightest idea what he had put his wife and children through for twelve years. I put him straight.

"Suddenly, you're self-righteous because you're here three months. You think you've changed and feel ready to go home. What do you have to offer? You have nothing to counter all the damage you did. As a matter of fact, you should be praising your wife that she has stood with you this long."

This man's wife was honest about how she felt. She loved him and knew that hiding the truth about the damage he'd done wouldn't help anyone. True love tells the truth. "I really love you. I don't trust you yet, but I love you."

No truth? No change.

Too many times people lie or hold back in order to keep the peace because they are afraid of losing their loved one. In my experience, those who are honest have more positive results than those who compromise.

Years ago, there was a TV game show called *Truth or Consequences.* The desire to change will come when your loved one is faced with both. Sometimes, tough love requires the truth and consequence of calling the police. In the next chapter, we'll talk about when you should involve law enforcement for your loved one's greater good and when you shouldn't.

What are you willing to do to save your loved one's life? Calling 911 may be the wake-up call they need. It may save their life.

NEW LIFE SUCCESS STEPS

+ If possible, avoid talking with your loved one if they are high or if you are physically exhausted. Substances and fatigue can both undermine emotions and sabotage your efforts.

+ Approach your loved one in love, calmly, and with a respectful tone.

+ Seek Christian counseling individually and as a family. The perspective of a professional with experience in this area will give you a new outlook on the situation, provide fresh insights, and offer ways to move forward while developing new patterns in the family dynamic.

+ Be aware of others who might be impacted in a positive way by what you are trying to teach your addicted loved one

+ Be honest—always.

+ Be willing to make the hard, beneficial choice—even if it hurts. The Bible says, in 1 Corinthians 13:6, that love *"rejoices not in iniquity, but rejoices in the truth."*

9

WHEN SHOULD I CALL THE POLICE?

"Give your emotions the time they need to accept the difficult
things your mind already understands."
—*Rosalinda Torres Rivera*

This is not a tragic tale. This is a true, courageous story of drastic measures taken.

Shaking, and with tears in my eyes, I dialed 911.

My hands were tied. My husband and I were at a loss. We had done everything we could think of, and yet, nothing had changed. We loved our girl. But if something were to happen, if we could've

stopped it and didn't, I…I just don't know how we would have survived it. We had no choice but to make the call.

No one who loves an addicted person wants to live through what this
woman and her husband lived through, but many would be better off today
if they had made the call. If you've ever loved an alcoholic or addict, you've
likely experienced the kind of nightmare described below.

The scene is still fresh in your mind, the one where the police come to
the door in the middle of the night. You bolt upright in bed at the sound of
the doorbell and race to answer the door. A police officer there. He speaks
in a calm, professional manner: "Are you Mr./Mrs. _____? I'm sorry to
have to inform you that your son/daughter/wife/husband/mother/father/
brother/sister was in a car accident/involved in a shooting/found unconscious at a party. I regret to inform you…."

I don't want to sound overly dramatic. I don't want to cause you more
pain or worry than you already endure. However, I do want to make sure
you understand the high risk of addiction. I want you to consider carefully
how far you would go to save your loved one. Are you willing to take the
necessary measures when drastic times call for them, like the woman who
dialed 911?

STEPHANIE'S MOTHER TELLS HER STORY

I'm raising my grandson because my daughter, Stephanie, isn't
capable of taking care of him. I don't want to have to look him in
the eyes and tell him his mother is gone. I don't want to have to
sit down and explain that *gone* doesn't mean *away for the weekend*.
I don't want to have to explain to this little boy that *dead* means
never coming back.

My husband and I talked it over and knew we had to call the police on our own daughter. I knew this was the only way to protect
her from herself. I clung to my faith in God, but while she was in
jail on drug charges, I often questioned if we did the right thing. I
thought she would never speak to us again, that we might lose her

forever. But in reality, we were going to lose her anyway, with no chance to make things right.

Stephanie was angry for a while. But after being in jail a few weeks, she started to feel better physically. Her mind became clearer. She still couldn't believe that her own parents called the cops on her, but over time, she accepted the fact that our motive in doing so was our love for her.

Stephanie and her parents talk about that day now. They talk about it because they *can* talk about it. They can drink iced tea while the kids play in the yard. They can talk about how Stephanie's parents saved her life by calling the police on her one night. They get to do those things because Stephanie is still alive.

We know beyond a doubt that one of the hardest choices we've had to make was the right choice. Ten years ago, I dialed 911 to report my child. Now she has been restored. She got married this past year. Her son stood up with my husband and gave her away at the altar. I thank God for giving us the strength to make the tough call. I can't remember the last time I had one of those nightmares.

I've spoken to many parents, relatives, and friends who have had to face the difficult decision of calling the police. It's not a decision any of them came to quickly or easily.

I'm sure there are people who call the police over minor issues because they don't want to deal with the brokenness of their relationships. There are neighbors who will send the cops to their house every time their teenager plays his music too loud. Calling the authorities on your addicted loved one is different. This is life or death. But how do you know when you've reached the point where that call could save them?

Calling the police, or delivering your friend or relative into police custody, can seem like an extreme over-the-top measure for some people. But it can be a life-saving measure. Many jails and prisons offer rehabilitation services behind bars, which can be the first step toward living free from addiction. It is a rational move for distressed friends and family who have tried everything else.

I realize that outside the U.S., there are countries and cultures in which the police are corrupt and extremely dangerous. Calling officials in those areas could be harmful. If you live in a location where reaching out to officials could be harmful, even deadly, you must take that into consideration when deciding whether or not to make that call. But in countries that do not exist under the reign of corrupt law enforcement, this can be a life-saving measure.

I firmly believe that no matter how much we care about someone, we have a responsibility for their safety and well-being. You might say, "I'm not my brother's keeper. My buddy can do his thing, and I'll do mine."

That's not love. That's not being a true friend. It's selfish. You can't afford to risk burying a friend or loved one because you decided to opt out. The consequences are too great to worry about what anyone will think just to avoid doing something difficult.

If we care like we say we do, we must be willing to prove it and take the risk. There may come a time when you are left with no good options. If your addicted loved one engages in a situation that causes someone to be in danger, including themselves, calling the police is the only decision that will defuse the situation.

THERE MAY COME A TIME WHEN YOU ARE LEFT WITH NO GOOD OPTIONS. IF YOUR ADDICTED LOVED ONE ENGAGES IN A SITUATION THAT CAUSES SOMEONE TO BE IN DANGER, INCLUDING THEMSELVES, CALLING THE POLICE IS THE ONLY DECISION THAT WILL DEFUSE THE SITUATION.

I have a friend who did prison time because his sister turned him in to the police. This was during my gang days in Brooklyn. This guy tried to hide his addiction but she caught him with his needle and confronted him. She didn't know what to do for him. She knew the drugs were dangerous. She knew the situation was bigger than she could handle.

The only thing she knew to do was to call the police and have him arrested. This was no in-and-out charge, either. Her brother ended up serving two-and-a-half years in prison.

When I spoke with him back then, he was angry. His only sister ratted on him and got him put away. Behind bars, however, there was no trouble to get into and he turned his life around. When he was released, he started his own company, and today, he lives a productive life. That woman saved her brother's life with a phone call.

We don't always want to call the police because we are trying to protect our loved one's reputation—or perhaps our own. Saving face may result in having to face our part in their death. Harsh, but true. We must care about the condition of others, even if it costs us something.

This is the case when it comes to friends not wanting to call for help when someone overdoses at a party. They panic and don't want anyone to get into trouble. Or they aren't inclined to call the cops if they're high themselves. Getting your friend into trouble is better than getting him in a casket. In cases of overdose, laws are changing to encourage witnesses to call for help without the risk of certain arrest themselves. These laws generally provide immunity from arrest, charge, or prosecution for certain controlled substance possession and paraphernalia offenses when a person who is either experiencing an opiate-related overdose or observing one calls 911 for assistance or seeks medical attention.[20]

We must make tough decisions, especially if we know our loved one is irrational and behaving recklessly. Don't minimize the danger when you know your loved one has come to the point of self-destruction or risk to others.

---

20. "Drug Overdose Immunity and Good Samaritan Laws," National Conference on State Legislatures, June 5, 2017, http://www.ncsl.org/research/civil-and-criminal-justice/drug-overdose-immunity-good-samaritan-laws.aspx (accessed August 28, 2018).

A man found his wife in an alcoholic stupor, bloodied and passed out in the middle of the street, blocks from their home. He wasn't able to move her and couldn't leave her there to be run over or attacked. He had to swallow his pride, disregard his wife's reputation, and call 911. Unfortunately, this wasn't the first time, or even the fifth time, he'd had to contact the police over his wife's drunken escapades.

Often, it is not a singular event that pushes us to move past our shame and embarrassment and reach out for emergency help. We know addictive behavior escalates over time, making the dangers greater and the consequences more severe.

Some drugs can cause a person to do crazy things, like becoming violent or engaging in high-risk activities. When I was on the streets using drugs every day, I had a connection who dealt drugs from his home. He was married and had three children. I remember seeing both the husband and the wife shoot up in front of their children. They did it as naturally as if they were drinking a beer or a soda. Even though I was an addict and under the influence of heroin, I knew that was nuts.

Looking back, I see how that couple committed a terrible crime. With that kind of example and living environment, the result was the same as if they had stuck a needle into the arms of their children and hooked them on heroin. If you know a child is in danger of being neglected because of a loved one's drug use or drinking, will you step up and call the police or social services?

Countless addicts have been charged with child endangerment. The students in our program tell stories of the times they put their children at risk because of their addiction. You see the shame on their faces when they share how they got high in front of their kids, allowed a drug dealer or complete strangers into their home, or left a baby in the car seat with the car running while they ran into a bar for "just one drink."

One graduate of the Mercy House went to jail after a man on a bike noticed her child asleep in the car. It was the dead of winter and this mom had gone into a bar. In her haze, she lost track of time. An officer came into the establishment looking for her and told the woman what time it was. After losing custody of her child, she decided she'd had enough and entered our program.

She's now sober and back with her husband and children. If it wasn't for one brave person getting involved and making a phone call, she would have received a more serious charge and her child would likely be dead. A child endangerment charge carries tremendous weight.

Even after having the opportunity to change and restore their relationships with their children, many addicts are no longer allowed to attend school functions because of their police record. Renting an apartment or securing certain jobs is difficult after charges are filed. Plus, lasting trauma can devastate a child.

Calling 911 probably proved easier for the cyclist because he didn't have a relationship with the person about whom he was calling. He didn't have to think about how this woman's reactions or feelings would affect him. He only cared about the child. In situations where you know the addict you're reporting, those considerations can cause us to hesitate to pick up the phone.

Personal concern can keep us from doing the right thing. But when a child is being neglected or put in danger, how could we hesitate to protect them? If your loved one has a child or a younger sibling, protection must be the priority.

Years ago, I was acquainted with a family who had a baby girl. When I went to visit them one day, the child smelled as if she hadn't had a diaper change for a week. I called out but no one was home. The baby was alone. I couldn't leave her there, so I took the little one to my mother. My mother went out of her mind when she saw the condition of this child. She kept her long enough to be washed and fed, then had to send the child back to my friends' place. Six weeks later, that baby was left alone in the house again. This time, a fire broke out, and the baby was trapped inside. She died. It changed my perspective forever.

Today, there are stricter laws. As a family member or friend, you need to be aware of them because they may affect you, especially if the addict is living under the same roof as a minor.

The article, "Parental Drug Use as Child Abuse," found on the Child Welfare Information Gateway website, says,

> There is increasing concern about the negative effects on children when parents or other members of their households abuse alcohol or drugs or engage in other illegal drug-related activity, such as the manufacture of methamphetamines in home-based laboratories. Many states have responded to this problem by expanding the civil definition of child abuse or neglect to include this concern. Specific circumstances that are considered child abuse or neglect in some states include:
>
> + Manufacturing a controlled substance in the presence of a child or on premises occupied by a child.
>
> + Exposing a child to, or allowing a child to be present where, chemicals or equipment for the manufacture of controlled substances are used or stored.
>
> + Selling, distributing, or giving drugs or alcohol to a child.
>
> + Using a controlled substance that impairs the caregiver's ability to adequately care for the child.
>
> + Exposing a child to the criminal sale or distribution of drugs....
>
> ...Nine states have enacted enhanced penalties for any conviction for the manufacture of methamphetamine when a child was on the premises where the crime occurred.
>
> Exposing children to the manufacture, possession, or distribution of illegal drugs is considered child endangerment in 11 states. In North Carolina and Wyoming, selling or giving an illegal drug to a child by any person is a felony.[21]

Other nations have, or are enacting, stringent laws regarding children's exposure to chemical substances. No matter where you live, it's important to be informed about the laws protecting the innocent. These are not

---

21. "Parental Drug Use as Child Abuse," Child Welfare Information Gateway, April 2015, https://www.childwelfare.gov/topics/systemwide/laws-policies/statutes/drugexposed/ (accessed August 28, 2018).

charges anyone should risk. We have moral and legal obligations to protect children living in the home of a substance abuser.

When addiction involves single-parent residences, step-parents, or multiple people living together under one roof, it is more complicated. It's important to treat each situation individually. Determine the addict's role in the family.

Adjusting your approach to finding help is essential when attempting to protect children or siblings from the problems. We have witnessed situations where a child needs to be removed from the home. The child may have one parent in jail while the other one is abusing substances. They might exhibit the same symptoms as the addict themselves: poor hygiene, inability to stay awake, low grades, or not attending school altogether. Whatever the signs, pay attention and protect the innocent when you can.

In our second phase women's home, Mercy Moms House, we have seen the power of forgiveness and restoration take place between mothers and their children. Healing *is* possible. Many of our moms and dads have criminal records but the courts allow them to come to New Life For Youth to learn how to be responsible parents and citizens. The involvement of the court system is added motivation for those young people who want to turn their lives around but need help to do so. With court mandates in place, addicts have more of a reason to stay substance-free, so their children can have normal, healthy lives.

It's not uncommon to hear stories of children forced to parent their moms or dads. With a parent debilitated by drug or alcohol use, many children are left to their own devices, shouldering more responsibilities than they should have to bear. They cook, making sure the parent and younger siblings eat. They do the homework, bathe younger siblings, and even help mommy with her drug paraphernalia so she doesn't become sick from withdrawals.

Children should be playing, growing, and learning. They should not be hiding things from Grandma or missing school to take care of Dad. They shouldn't have to lie and cover up their living conditions. They do these things because they don't want "the government lady in the white car" to come and take them away.

When children are affected by addiction, that's the only requirement you need to dial 911. We are all responsible for the future of our next generation. Knowing what a child is enduring and doing nothing about it is beyond unacceptable. If I didn't know the forgiveness of God, I might call it *unforgivable*. If left unchecked, such children often becomes the next addicts.

WHEN CHILDREN ARE AFFECTED BY ADDICTION, THAT'S THE ONLY REQUIREMENT YOU NEED TO DIAL 911. WE ARE ALL RESPONSIBLE FOR THE FUTURE OF OUR NEXT GENERATION. KNOWING WHAT A CHILD IS ENDURING AND DOING NOTHING ABOUT IT IS BEYOND UNACCEPTABLE.

Through the years, we have seen fathers and sons or mothers and daughters in our program simultaneously. We've had several sets of siblings go through, one after another, as the entire family got free from chemical dependency.

If you are the child who has been living with your parents' addiction, perhaps most of your life, ask the Lord for guidance. He will show you what to do in every situation—even if it's getting a responsible, caring adult to dial 911.

Having to call the authorities can be difficult, but saving a life is worth it. In 2015, drug overdoses driven by the heroin scourge, as well as prescription pain relievers such as oxycodone, hydrocodone, codeine, morphine, and fentanyl, were the leading cause of accidental death in the U.S., according to the American Society of Addiction Medicine. In that year, there were 20,101 fatal overdoses related to prescription painkillers and 12,990 stemming from heroin.[22]

How far will you go to save your loved one's life? You've been given a lot of heavy information in this chapter, and some sad, scary examples. My hope is that calling the police won't be necessary for you. Continue to implement the strategies you're learning in each of these chapters. Rely on God and pray for Him to change your loved one's heart and mind. That change may come and you may never have to make that difficult decision to dial 911. But if you do, a basic understanding of what the law allows always helps.

Most laws won't let you force an adult loved one into a program unless it is a psychiatric center. Even then, you need to go before a judge and prove that the individual is in danger or endangering the lives of others. If the addict is a juvenile, you may have more options, but even then, the action could require a court order.

According to the Society for Adolescent Medicine, many states in the U.S. accord minors limited autonomy to provide consent for treatment of sensitive and private issues, such as pregnancy, sexually transmitted diseases, and drug, alcohol, or mental health problems. Where applicable, this act leaves a parent or guardian powerless.[23]

I have discovered the best way to get help for a loved one is to talk to them from your heart. Convince them through persistent insistence, pressing the issue and bathing the conversation in lots of patience and love. There is no guarantee they will see the need to get help. Reminding them of what addiction has cost them, and painting a mental image of their happy, successful future, can help them envision the life they desire. I recommend straightforward questions like these:

+ "Do you want help?"
+ "What do you want for your life?"

22. "Opioid Addiction 2016 Facts & Figures," American Society of Addiction Medicine, https://www.asam.org/docs/default-source/advocacy/opioid-addiction-disease-facts-figures.pdf (accessed August 28, 2018).
23. Sigman G, Silber TJ, English A, Epner JE, "Confidential health care for adolescents: position paper of the Society for Adolescent Medicine," *The Journal of Adolescent Health*, December, 21, 1997, (6):408–15.

+ "What are you willing to do to get it?"

+ "What are you willing to lose to make it happen?"

Their initial response may push for a compromise that leans in their advantage. Addiction is not going to go down without a fight. But you have a lot of fight in you. Stay strong. Your loved one's life is not negotiable.

The Bible reminds us in Romans 6:23, *"For the wages of sin is death; but the gift of God is eternal life through Jesus Christ our Lord."*

If you are not a believer in God's willingness to help you reach your loved one, I hope your heart yearns for the power available to you through a relationship with Jesus. Because Christ died for us on the cross, we can experience freedom from our sins, not only from our past poor choices, but also from those temptations we face in the present. Whatever we have done, no matter how we may have failed, there is freedom and forgiveness in Jesus Christ.

You've probably figured out that not everyone has your back on this journey to freedom. Even family members can undermine progress. In our next chapter, we'll talk through strategies for navigating disagreements. Not everyone is on the same page when it comes to dealing with your addicted loved one.

NEW LIFE SUCCESS STEPS

+ Be willing to dial 911. It's better that your loved one expresses their anger at you than to give in and lose them forever.

+ If possible, remove children from unsafe environments.

+ Be willing to go to court to help minor children find the help they need.

+ Believe in God, who will strengthen you. When everything and everyone around you fails, trust in God, because He will never fail you.

+ When authorities, professionals, and others in power disregard your pleas for help, but you know the situation has reached critical mass, dial 911 again. Do not let anyone deter you from acting when needed.

10

WHAT SHOULD I DO WHEN OTHERS DISAGREE ON HOW TO DEAL WITH MY LOVED ONE'S ADDICTION?

"The will of God will not take us where the grace of God cannot sustain us."
—*Billy Graham*

In this battle, some of the most devastating attacks come from "friendly fire." Family and friends can disagree on how to approach your loved one's addiction and treatment options. They can add to your stress instead of supporting you. I know you were expecting, or at least hoping, that everyone would see the situation as clearly as you do and eagerly jump on board with your plan, but now you're feeling that was unrealistic. It's rarely that easy.

Let's face it, we all have relationships with at least one person with whom we've never seen eye to eye. Ever. On any subject. It seems that every interaction with them is harder than it needs to be. Why should agreeing on how to save your loved one from a murderous addiction be any different? You would think it would be easy to rally together in this case, but, well, the ties that bind us sometimes *bind us*.

Before we do anything else, let's talk about family structure and how to move beyond tolerance, in which we turn differences to our advantage in winning this battle over addiction. And there are plenty of differences among us.

FAMILY DYNAMICS

If you were to gather together all the significant people in your addicted loved one's life, your dining room table would probably include many of the following characters. See if you can identify them:

+ Those who can't see the bad.
+ Those who can't see the good.
+ Those who can't forgive.
+ Those who can't stop being a doormat.
+ Those who can do no wrong.
+ Those who play the scapegoat.
+ Those who can't say no.
+ Those who argue about everything.
+ Those who refuse to get involved.
+ Those who refuse to let go of control.
+ Those who don't care enough to show up.
+ Those who will never give up.

You are the one who picked up this book. You are determined to see your loved one free. You are being trained. You are holding out hope above everything else. You can help your friends and family do the same. But before that can happen, the family has to move past their common roles for the sake of the common goal.

Most families are complicated and messy, because human beings are complicated and messy. We all have our issues, in one way or another. Throw my unique brand of "complicated" in with someone else's brand of "complicated" and get ready for some bumpy moments, even when addiction isn't thrown into the mix.

FAMILIAL DISAGREEMENTS

You and your family have been doing life together for a long time. We love our families, but that doesn't mean we love everything about everyone all the time. This is universal in every relationship. Families argue and disagree. One or more of your family members are still holding on to events from the past. There may be unforgiveness and bitterness over some wrong-doing. Or it may be as simple as a group of different people with opposing personalities, diverse goals, and conflicting agendas, all trying to exist together. We don't all share the same views, so we try to convince others to see things our way. We debate and try to win others to our side.

Everyone has hot buttons. In an urgent situation with someone you all love, you can guarantee a few people are going to get theirs pushed. What are yours? Maybe you're looking into a long-term treatment facility that will provide your loved one with a better chance at lifelong sobriety. Someone else feels your loved one needs to do thirty days so they can get back to work and support their family.

Prepare for group clashes over everything. Prepare to encounter different perspectives on the severity of the addiction, on religious beliefs, on parenting, and on the life choices of everyone involved. If you're at the place of deciding on a course of treatment, you and your family, friends, and possibly your loved one's coworkers will disagree here, too.

+ How long should they be in treatment?
+ Where should they go?
+ When?
+ Who is paying for this? (That's a big one.)

In the healthiest of families, money issues cause enormous stress on relationships. In the case of addiction, your loved one, more than likely, has caused a lot of expense already, and some of your family members may not be willing to dole out any more cash. That is what Rene was up against with her family after her husband's relapse.

RENE'S STORY

Rene, like you, had spent endless hours worrying, praying, and hoping that Tom, her husband, would realize the severity of his condition and get help. When his epiphany finally came, Rene was thrilled—her prayers had been answered. She was also overwhelmed. Tom was finally ready to get help, but she didn't know where the money was going to come from. As with many addicts, Tom had burned many bridges through his addiction. He'd made a lot of promises, borrowed a lot of money, and failed to repay loans, more than once.

Desperate to grab the chance while she could, Rene made phone calls to Tom's previous debtors, begging them to reach into their pockets again. Her husband's life depended on getting him into treatment. It didn't go well. Doors were slammed in Rene's face. She was cussed out at the grocery store. So many people hung up on her that Rene started to feel like a telemarketer.

Finally, she turned to her brother, thinking he would come to her rescue again. As she turned into his driveway, he stormed out of the front door, not even giving Rene the opportunity to get out of the car. "No!" he shouted. "Uh-uh. Not this time. We're done, Rene. I'm sorry."

Family members, friends, and even Tom's old hunting buddies all were unwilling to trust him again. He'd been in rehab three times. Why should they believe this time would end differently? Friends demanded proof he was going to go through with it. They wanted a money-back guarantee that it would stick. The only assurance Rene could make was that if they did nothing and Tom didn't get help, he would end up dead within a year.

Finally, Tom's nephew agreed to send a check, with the understanding that it was the last time he was going to help. Rene knew Tom had better do the work.

It may seem as though Tom and Rene's families are filled with horrible, awful, selfish people. I don't believe that's true. You and I have lived through addiction, and we've seen what it does to the people in our lives. As much as we know our loved one needs help, we also have to admit to understanding how people feel hesitant to help after being cheated and lied to so many times.

For the most part, Tom's story has a happy ending. After completing a year-long program, he has been clean and sober for several years now. Many family ties have been mended, but not all of them. Some people still won't forgive his past. Rebuilding trust requires a lot of time and proof. Restoration means forgiveness must flow both ways.

Rene still struggles to forgive some of her family for the way they responded to her cries for help. As often happens in the middle of tension, pain, and frustration, emotions took over. It got ugly. You may know exactly what that is like.

We are in a battle with the forces *behind* addiction. But we can't win the war if we are dodging friendly fire and fighting against the people who should be in the fight with us. Let's stop taking aim in anger. For the sake of the family and other relationships, we must not turn on each other. We can disagree without destroying people.

When you gather to discuss your addiction situation, set ground rules for effective communication. Your family dynamic may require you to make additions or adjustments, but make sure everyone understands and agrees to specific expectations when going into group conversations.

FIGHT FAIR

+ Don't make honesty an excuse for personal attacks.

+ Don't cast blame.

+ Don't bully others into sharing your view.

+ Stay away from hot buttons. Don't push known sensitive areas and don't react when yours are pushed. Family and close friends are often expert button-pressers. Play well with others.

+ Do not berate or belittle another person's opinion. Commit to respectful comments.

+ Recognize which opinions are important to challenge and which ones are not that crucial. Choose your battles. Don't get caught up in insignificant grievances. Check yourself moment by moment.

+ Guard against absolute statements:

"You always…"

"He never…"

"Every time I try to…"

"All you do is…"

"Everyone is against me…"

"Everything is…"

REMEMBER THAT YOU LOVE EACH OTHER

How do you move forward when you don't seem to agree on much of anything? You find the things you *do* agree on. When you realize you're going around and around in circles, and when reconciling your differences seems impossible, stop. Just stop. Let everyone take a minute to breathe and shift the spotlight.

When we focus on what we don't agree on, those conflicts can steal our attention away from what's really important—delivering our loved one to wholeness and a healthy life without substance abuse. We can forget that the ultimate goal is to see the entire family healed.

How do you get back on track? You sort it out the same way detectives do.

If you've ever watched a crime drama on television, you know any good investigation sends police detectives to canvass the neighborhood. Law enforcement goes door to door, house to house, to get information from anyone who may have witnessed the incident. Different descriptions and details come from the witnesses. We wonder how law enforcement will ever figure out the who-done-it. The information the cops scribble in their notebooks is so varied, how do they ever sort out proof from perception? They need what *we* need to achieve unity. In the end, investigators arrive at the truth by looking at the intersections of eyewitness accounts. They filter out the differences in the stories and focus on the similarities.

This is how you will come to a mutual truth and achieve a united front with those who see your loved one's addiction situation differently. Set aside what you don't agree on. Resume your conversation from a place of truth. What do you agree on as evidenced by proof? Where's your place of common ground?

Even if you don't agree on how to make healing happen, or even if it can, the common goal of wanting to see your loved one free of addiction can help you make progress. Keep that as your foundation and the catalyst for finding an answer. Building from a strong place of mutual care and love for the addict can keep things from crumbling later.

You don't have to agree with an opposing point of view to respect a person's right to have it. And if you respect and consider each other's input, you may find a new way to come at this addiction.

The Bible describes Christians as being part of the body of Christ. First Corinthians describes various parts of the body, all with different yet valid and important functions. It says that one body part shouldn't despise the others for having a different purpose.

All of them will take care of one another. If one part suffers, every part suffers with it. If one part is honored, every part shares in its joy."
(1 Corinthians 12:25–26 NIrV)

Remember, addiction is a family issue. Everyone is impacted. It will take a unified group to complete this mission. Being the same is not required for unification. Our differences were never meant to divide us. As we learn to respect each other, showing gratitude for what each member brings to the table, those different talents and experiences can be integrated into the solution your loved one needs.

We must determine and commit to letting everyone else in this group of diverse personalities think and respond in their own way. Everyone comes to the journey with their own set of ideas and values, levels of understanding, and expectations of how your loved one will behave going forward.

FOCUSED DETERMINATION

Expectations are forged from education and experience. We expect to see what we have always seen. The sun comes up and goes down, and we aren't shocked when it happens. The world is turning as it always has and always will, until the day God wants to do something different. We expect the sun will set tonight because our experience tells us it will.

Your loved one has caused people to expect certain things. They have been consistent in their inconsistency. Some look at the addicted loved one with the same expectancy as we do the rising sun. Always has—always will. Cut them some slack. They don't know what you know. They don't have your hope. Some will come around. Others may not. Some will be all-in while others may not want any part of helping you reach your loved one. It's a predictable pattern.

My uncle, my father's brother, was the pastor of a large church. When my mother went to the family for help, his first reaction was to have me put away. He looked at my mother and said, "There's no hope for Victor. He is a drug addict, a druggie on the streets. He will never change."

Though my uncle didn't help my mother, he did offer something. He said, "I'll help you go through all the necessary steps to put him away somewhere. Face it, there is no hope for your son."

Can you imagine how my mother felt? Reaching out only to be turned down?

You may not have to imagine it. You may have had a similar experience. Sometimes, the people you least expect turn their backs on you. My mother and father thought my uncle would surely step up. He was a pastor! But he offered no help and no hope.

Unfortunately, the greatest opposition often comes from family, friends, coworkers, and even people of faith. But God hasn't given up. Put your hope in Him, not in people.

FAMILY DELIVERANCE

Every individual makes their own choice. But I will tell you from my experience in addiction and more than forty-five years in addiction treatment, there is a divine domino effect that starts with you and your addicted loved one, then makes its way through your entire family, especially when you stand on God's promises to restore the broken. God wants restoration for you and your family.

IF YOUR FAMILY ISN'T COMPLETELY ON BOARD WITH YOUR BELIEF IN YOUR LOVED ONE'S POTENTIAL DELIVERANCE, KEEP PRAYING AND BELIEVING. KEEP DOING WHAT YOU KNOW IS RIGHT. AND DON'T GIVE UP ON THOSE WHO OPPOSE YOUR HOPE.

I have seen young men and women come into our program with little family support. On their first visit, nobody shows up to support them. When it comes time for their first pass, no one comes. Then, little by little, as the months pass by, I am introduced to new family members. As the students begin to change, their loved ones are drawn in. Twelve months later, someone who couldn't even get a family member to answer the phone on call day, has four rows full of supporters at their graduation.

This is not a rare occurrence. This is the norm when God is involved, because He doesn't do anything halfway. If your family isn't completely on board with your belief in your loved one's potential deliverance, keep praying and believing. Keep doing what you know is right. And don't give up on those who oppose your hope, the same way you haven't given up on your addicted loved one.

FAITHFUL DURING THE DELAY

Whether your inner circle agrees or not, let me encourage you to look for support from people who *are* in agreement with your recovery solutions. Link up with people who know what you're going through. It can be discouraging when those closest to the situation don't get involved, but a large community who believe in the transformation process exists. You can find support.

Reaching out to strangers might seem awkward at first. Walking into a room full of unknown faces can be intimidating. But it won't take long for you to develop relationships that will lift and strengthen you. The positivity you receive will help you stand against any negative forces trying to drag you down. You'll be able to release painful emotions, knowing you have someone in your corner. Whether it's family, friends, or a new group of like-minded supporters, you can always count on the Holy Spirit to be there.

The Bible tells us, *"But the Comforter, which is the Holy Ghost, whom the Father will send in My name, He shall teach you all things, and bring all things to your remembrance, whatsoever I have said to you"* (John 14:26).

As you rely on God, who is always faithful and has your back, whether anyone else shows up or not, you will have everything you need. Build your hope on Him. Make God your rock, and you will stand strong.

Wherever you find yourself in this situation, ask God for patience with the healing process and other people. In what can seem like a lonely place, your faith will be tested, as will your love for your loved one. People may turn their backs on you. What seemed like a lot of support in the beginning may dwindle, as those who tire from the fight drop out.

Know this and stand confident: you are not alone. Find other people with faith like yours who will help and encourage you. The solid rock of Jesus's love will sustain you when those closest to you turn away. Be willing to do whatever it takes to see your loved one leave their life of pain and addiction. You may feel like you're going crazy at times, but as we'll discuss in the next chapter, addiction needn't drive you to the loony bin.

NEW LIFE SUCCESS STEPS

+ Make the decision that you are in it for the long haul. The battle will take time. Brace yourself and gear up for the fight.

+ Don't let family influence you to extremes. Some will say, "Give up. They're too far gone." Others will try to convince you you're overreacting, saying, "It's just a little pot or beer." Stick with what you know and stand your ground.

+ Seek to understand the perspective of others. If you want others to hear what you have to say, first listen to them.

+ Back up your beliefs with facts. Be able to prove what you've learned in this book and elsewhere.

+ Bring credible resources to support your beliefs if you need backup.

+ Don't be divided by differences. When you disagree with others in your addicted loved one's life, focus on this common ground: you love him or her and want to see them free.

+ Connect to a support group or church. Don't do life alone. Find others who have gone through similar struggles and overcome them. A fantastic resource is *Celebrate Recovery*. (See Appendix.)

+ Don't expect others to have the same faith you do. Prepare yourself for opposition.

+ Be patient. God hasn't forgotten you.

11

I FEEL LIKE I'M GOING CRAZY.
AM I?

"Life is like a roller coaster, you can either close your eyes and
scream, or choose to focus on moments to enjoy."
—*Unknown*

Let me put your mind at ease from the start. You're not going mad. You just happen to love an addict. Those two things do feel a lot alike. But no, you're not going crazy. Here's what you have to realize—addiction is not rational.

If you don't understand addiction, you will try to decipher your loved one's behavior based on reasonable, rational thinking. This doesn't work. It will feel like you're going crazy because *addiction doesn't make sense*. It's not rational. And it especially doesn't make sense when you don't understand what it is you are dealing with, when you aren't sure you can believe your eyes most of the time.

If you've accepted that your loved one's an addict, or if you suspect they are, you've stepped into a strange new world. When you're not acquainted with a new culture, nothing in it seems familiar. The game of addiction isn't normal for you. The addict's world can feel so disorienting and disappointing that you can start to question your own grip on reality. A person you've known their whole life can suddenly become unrecognizable.

When nothing your loved one tells you makes any sense, it can become easy to believe them and doubt yourself. You begin to wonder if you're really seeing what you think you see. It's confusing, and you can end up feeling like *you* are the one with the problem.

I've been where you are. Parents, children, spouses, and friends in households all around the world are going through exactly what you are going through right now. There are universal commonalities for anyone who cares for a person lost in the lifestyle of addiction. Addiction has its own methods and patterns. Regardless of the type of addiction, each has certain characteristics, stages, and behaviors that are predictable.

UNDERSTANDING THE PATTERNS OF BEHAVIOR IN ADDICTS CAN HELP YOU MAKE SENSE OF THE SENSELESS. AWARENESS KEEPS YOU STEADY AND PREPARES YOU TO BATTLE AGAINST THE ADDICTION THAT HOLDS YOUR LOVED ONE HOSTAGE.

Addiction thrives on chaos and destruction. The consequences of addiction destroy our loved ones, their relationships, and anything good and worthwhile in their lives. The more disorder and confusion in their relationships, the more separation and isolation there is. The deeper the addict goes into chemical dependency, the further things spin out of control.

When addiction's at play, there's a lot of deception in your present reality, a lot of emotions, physical changes, value-system shifts, and erratic behavior. This is common in the world of addiction. Understanding the patterns of behavior in addicts can help you make sense of the senseless. Awareness keeps you steady and prepares you to battle against the addiction that holds your loved one hostage.

Hosea 4:6 says, *"My people are destroyed for lack of knowledge."* Let me encourage you. You are doing the right thing by gathering knowledge. You are collecting ammunition and being trained in how to use it against the forces of addiction. The more information you gain about what's happening to your loved one, the more confident you will become.

I can't emphasize this point enough: don't take anything for granted. There will be times when you need every bit of knowledge you've gathered in order to save your addicted loved one from the grip of this enemy. Managing your own emotions is going to be one of your most difficult tasks.

Relationships are complex. Throw substance abuse into the mix and *complex* turns into *catastrophic*. I know a couple who has dealt with their twenty-four-year-old daughter's alcoholism for several years. She lives with them and they have done everything they can to get her sober. Ongoing tension lives with them, too. Every area of their life is affected. Their nerves are wearing thin. It has become harder and harder to keep rising emotions in check. Anger and resentment seethe beneath the surface, waiting for one wrong look or comment that permits them to break out.

This couple tag-team their adult daughter in the same way we'd expect the parents of a toddler to share responsibilities. When the husband has a bad day at work, the wife keeps their daughter occupied. When the wife reaches her limit with the girl, the husband swoops in and runs interference. It's like dealing with a toddler, only with a larger, louder vocabulary, and more strength to slam doors, pound walls, and throw things.

On one of those high-anxiety days that has become the rule rather than the exception, Mom gave Dad *the look*. Maybe you've seen the look.

Maybe you've worn the look. With no words spoken, it says, *If you don't get her away from me right now, one of us is packing a bag.*

In one altercation, Dad attempted to diffuse the situation and lessen the tension between mother and daughter. He took his daughter into the yard to help him water the garden. This should have deescalated things, right? Not so fast. Minutes later, the daughter burst into the kitchen, pointed through the window to her father, and yelled, "That man is crazy!"

She had pushed his hot button. Dad lost it. Looking through the window at her normally laid-back, quiet husband, Mom saw a red face, arms waving wildly in the air, and lawn furniture in the pool. He looked like a madman.

How can you know if you are in danger of going too far?

WARNING SIGNS YOU MAY BE LOSING CONTROL

Your job or schoolwork is suffering.

Your mind is in other places. You are missing work or school to deal with the consequences of your addicted loved one's choices. Coworkers or teachers continually ask if you're okay. You have trouble concentrating and finishing projects.

Your finances are suffering.

Money spent on cleaning up your loved one's messes can take a toll on your financial accounts. Does your bank or credit card statement show entries for expenses like legal fees, property damage repairs, or making restitution for the consequences of their behavior? Are you missing money because they've stolen outright from you? The sin of addiction is costly.

Your health is suffering.

The bags under your eyes tell the story. Your stomach is always in knots. Losing sleep and not eating right because of stress and worry is impacting your general health. Your focus is on your addicted love one, causing you to neglect your own health and well-being. Do you break down and cry at the strangest moments? Not sleeping or keeping your body properly fueled will add to the already high toll on emotional and mental health. No wonder you feel like you're going crazy. Thankfully, you can make small changes to improve your health. We will get to that.

Your relationships are suffering.

When we are wounded or embarrassed, we isolate ourselves. Fear of what people will think of you or your family, because of your loved one's addiction, can make you want to hide. It's a natural response. Maybe your relationships are strained because you and others don't see eye to eye on how your situation should be handled. Maybe you're reading this and thinking that this point doesn't apply to you anymore because you don't have any outside relationships left. If that's where you are, you don't have to stay there. Keep reading.

Your family is suffering.

No one is left untouched when a loved one is an addict. Not only do you have your own emotions to deal with, but the anger and resentment from other family members affects you, too. Even though you all love the addicted person, your opinions about how to help them may be in opposition. Other family members can feel ignored. Children, especially, can feel neglected when all the attention seems to be focused on whatever fire needs to be put out next.

Your relationship with God is suffering.

You are trying so hard to be the savior in the life of your loved one that you neglect your own interaction with the actual Almighty God. Perhaps you have a dependency issue of your own—depending on yourself and not on God.

NOT NORMAL...BUT NOT HEALTHY

All these areas are impacted by what you deal with, day in and day out. It is normal. It is common. But it is not healthy. How you respond to these struggles is important for your loved one's freedom, your family's security, and your happiness and sanity. We'll cover steps to alleviate some of these difficulties so you can grow stronger in the process. Also, hold on to this promise for added strength: *"For God has not given us the spirit of fear; but of power, and of love, and of a sound mind"* (2 Timothy 1:7).

Even during outrageous moments and your own struggles to maintain your sanity, know that nothing we go through is pointless. No experience is useless or wasted. Of course, no one wants to have to go through what you're going through. Still, you can gain something positive in the middle of the madness. Knowing that may keep you from spinning out of control.

NO EXPERIENCE IS USELESS OR WASTED. OF COURSE, NO ONE WANTS TO HAVE TO GO THROUGH WHAT YOU'RE GOING THROUGH. STILL, YOU CAN GAIN SOMETHING POSITIVE IN THE MIDDLE OF THE MADNESS. KNOWING THAT MAY KEEP YOU FROM SPINNING OUT OF CONTROL.

In the book of Romans, we're reminded that all the things we're up against make us stronger in specific ways and increments: *"Tribulation works patience; and patience, experience; and experience, hope: and hope makes not ashamed"* (Romans 5:3–5).

Maybe you know the Bible as God's Word. Maybe you're not convinced about this "God thing." Regardless of your position right now, you can still look at this in a practical way. The Bible is a spiritual book, yes, and powerful, but it is also very sensible.

Look at the logical, practical results the verse from Romans reveals. We can get through the tough times we go through when we remember the following:

+ The difficulties of your hardest struggles build patience and endurance within you.

+ Trials help you get the hang of sticking it out when you feel like giving up.

+ Endurance strengthens your character when you learn not to panic or push.

+ When forced to wait and see, you're taught to rest a little before you see results. God's definition of faith is seeing and believing in your heart, even though you can't see it with your eyes. Yet.

Change takes time. This awful thing you're having to endure will leave you stronger when it's over. But the waiting can be maddening.

As we walk the addiction journey, it's easy to let our feelings get the best of us, causing us to lash out at our loved one. One of the most challenging statements God ever made comes from Psalm 46:10: *"Be still, and know that I am God."*

As I've said before, remember who your enemy is. It is not your loved one. No matter how they act, they are not your enemy, and you cannot behave like you are their enemy. In truth, you are not dealing with a flesh-and-blood enemy at all. You are up against *"rulers, against the authorities, against the powers of this dark world and against the spiritual forces of evil in the heavenly realms"* (Ephesians 6:12 NIV).

Addiction is a weapon. It's a weapon formed by the enemy to take everything your loved one has. The Bible says, *"The thief comes not, but for to steal, and to kill, and to destroy"* (John 10:10).

To combat confusion and wage the right battles, you first must make sure you are clear on who our enemy is. Then you can know how to defeat him. This clarity is as important for spiritual warfare as it is in the natural world. But this enemy can't be defeated in the usual way. If the enemy is spiritual, then it stands to reason that the only effective weapons to take him down must be spiritual. *"For the weapons of our warfare are not carnal, but mighty through God to the pulling down of strong holds"* (2 Corinthians 10:4).

The bottom line is, if you're attacking your loved one, you're letting the real enemy escape. Fear and guilt are weapons. If you let them control you,

you will end up like my friend, throwing yard furniture where yard furniture was never meant to be.

That same buddy of mine, when talking about his alcoholic daughter, would say that sometimes, he hated her. He experienced such guilt and sadness over how angry he was that it muddled his emotions. He would say, "I love her so much I hate her."

He didn't realize it immediately, but finally, he came to realize that his hatred was for *alcoholism* and what it had done to their family. He did not hate his daughter.

Years later, when his daughter was clean and sober, she went to her dad to ask his forgiveness for everything she had put him through. He hugged her and told her he kept no account of her wrongs. Then he asked *her* to forgive him for some of his mistakes.

My friend's daughter is sober to this day, and their family is whole. No more screaming, no more slamming doors, and no more floating lawn furniture. Those crazy times are over.

KEEP LEARNING AND TAKING STEPS.
KNOWLEDGE IS POWER, AND YOU'RE PLUGGING
IN. NOW THAT YOU ARE EDUCATED, YOU CAN
IDENTIFY THE SIGNS AND SAY TO YOURSELF,
*THIS IS REALLY HAPPENING. THIS ISN'T
SOMETHING I'M JUST IMAGINING.*

There it is—another reason to hope. Your day will come, though if you're reading this chapter, that day hasn't come for you yet. Keep learning and taking steps. Knowledge is power, and you're plugging in. Now that you are educated, you can identify the signs and say to yourself, *This is really happening. This isn't something I'm just imagining.* The following warning signs can also provide clarity.

WARNING SIGNS IN THE BEHAVIOR OF YOUR ADDICTED LOVED ONE

False promises of reform.

Addicts are manipulative. If you think your loved one would never lie to you, you may be right. They may have previously acted with full integrity, but addiction does not act with integrity—it keeps secrets and it lies. This is what controls an addict's behavior, and sometimes, your own. They will make promises of change to get you off their backs.

"I'm really trying."

"I'm really going to quit this time. You'll see."

"You know what, honey? Things are going to be different."

They may actually mean what they are saying. They may be 100 percent sincere. Maybe they've had some negative consequences that seem like rock bottom. But the minute they have the opportunity, sorry to say, they will break that promise for another high.

Addiction is stronger than you think.

Sometimes, it will feel like their addiction is greater than their love for you. Don't fail to exercise cautious optimism and patience. Hope for the change. But be on guard until you see the transformation.

Changes in sleeping patterns.

Day becomes night and night becomes day. Maybe your loved one goes days on end without sleeping and then crashes for a week. Drugs disturb sleep cycles. Alcohol can do the same. Opiate addiction causes nodding off, even in public.

Let me explain this term of *nodding*. Nodding is not falling asleep. It is similar to when a baby becomes limp and has no control over his body, as fatigue covers him like a blanket. He can't keep his eyes open or hold his head. He may fall from where he is sitting or standing.

In an opioid addict, this type of nodding is the effect of the chemicals on their brain. They can go on like this for hours, passing out and waking up, over and over. When you know what to look for, you will recognize it as the result of drug use, not of being sleepy.

Unable to keep a job/school issues.

Because of the other effects listed, eventually, work or school performance slips. Grades and attendance suffer. However, some addicts are able to hold down a steady job, depending on their addiction and the requirements of the job.

I remember a radio announcer who came through our program. She had been snorting cocaine off CDs every day, the entire time she was on the air. No one at the station knew. Her coworkers didn't know; her listeners didn't know. If she'd had to sit at a desk and answer phones, she couldn't have done it because she wouldn't have been able to hide her addiction so well. But this profession worked against her, allowing her to hide her cocaine addiction for years. It finally caught up to her when she went on a few benders and forgot to show up to work. Addiction's bill always comes due, sooner or later.

Out with the old friends, in with the new.

This is a big one. Do you find yourself asking questions like, "Hey, I haven't seen Tommy lately. Are you guys still friends?" The people your loved one used to spend time with are suddenly nowhere to be found. Is there a parade of new people coming through your house or picking up your loved one to "go hang out"? I used to introduce a new *friend* to my mother every day.

When fighting the war of addiction, you are not going crazy. You do need to resolve not to go down without a fight. When you've reached the point of acknowledging that your loved one has radically changed and is hardly recognizable, the signs will reveal the reality of the situation. But you have to be able to recognize it. Don't explain it away in your mind. Don't brush it under the rug. Investigate. You are the person who knows best when something is off. You are the person who loves them enough to fight this battle for them until they're ready to fight it for themselves.

Until that day, keep yourself grounded in the truth. Find your strength in the Lord.

THE REWARDS OF A PRAYER LIFE

In my opinion, a key weapon in this battle is prayer. Pray to reach your loved one and pray to keep them. I speak from firsthand experience. This is something my parents, especially my mother, never ceased to do. She constantly prayed for me.

My mom placed my name on many prayer lists around the city. She made me famous in heaven and on earth. Everywhere she went, she shared her burdens with other Christians and talked about the battle she was fighting as she tried to reach me.

My mom paid a great price by sacrificing much of her time. It was not easy. Her dedication and devotion paid off when my breakthrough came. Even after my life was changed, she continued to pray and share her victory and hope with others. She never lost her boldness or wavered in her drive to believe that God would change my life. Her prayer life not only affected me, it also affected the entire family, especially my dad. During the time of my addiction, he was not going to church and was on the cold side when it came to the things of God.

My brother and sister also benefited from her tenacious prayer life. Ultimately, my mother became a great source of strength and hope to many other parents struggling and fighting the fight for their own children.

It is equally important that you pray without ceasing on behalf of your all your loved ones. Prayer harnesses more power than all the other forces on earth. *"Then shall you call upon Me, and you shall go and pray to Me, and I will hearken to you"* (Jeremiah 29:12).

One day, everything you've been hoping for will come to pass. One day, your loved one will see that they want more than addiction can offer. When that day comes, you will want to know what to look for in a treatment program. Those tips are in our next chapter.

NEW LIFE SUCCESS STEPS

- Find a good friend to share your burden with. Resist the urge to isolate. Develop a support system to share your struggles and help you carry the weight of this crazy life.

- Listen to the voice of the Holy Spirit. God gave us a counselor. Let Him help you.

- Keep your head when others are losing theirs. Remember that sometimes you must wait before you see. Don't panic. Don't push.

- Prayer changes things. You may not be familiar with prayer, but we all know how to have a conversation. That's what prayer is. You know how to talk to a friend. That is what Jesus is for you.

- Stay positive. With so many things pulling you this way and that, keep your focus on gratitude in every moment.

12

WHAT SHOULD I LOOK FOR IN A TREATMENT PROGRAM?

"Desperate addiction requires heroic treatment."
—*Unknown*

You've been at odds with your loved one. The "No way!" you've heard for so long has finally shifted to "Yes. I'll get help. I don't want to live like this anymore."

First, decide what kind of treatment foundation you're looking for. If you want a faith-based program, you'll need one that does not compromise on Scripture. Any effective program should offer a whole-person approach: spiritual, mental, emotional, and physical. Remember, addiction, at its foundation, is a *spiritual* problem. There will be negotiables and non-negotiables as you and your loved one research options, but avoiding the spiritual aspect cannot be one of them.

TREATMENT CONSIDERATIONS

Once you have a list of possibilities, find out what each treatment program offers. The following sections address a variety of considerations that will be important to your loved one's recovery.

1. Will it get at the root cause of addiction?

Will the program deal only with the addiction and its symptoms, or will it help your loved one address the root causes, head-on? Will it dig deep or just put a bandage on the problem?

An effective program will confront your loved one with the real issue, the heart of their matter. It's not enough to cut off some branches. It's not even enough to chop down the tree at its base. If you don't get to the root, the problem will just grow back. Addiction is not a branch or a symptom. The core of addiction lies deep down in the roots. That's why any recovery program must deal with the heart, soul, body, and mind. It needs to consider the total person.

It will take more than a month or two to reach the deep root of spiritual issues.

2. What is the length of the program?

There are some who will be so fed up with their lives, they will determinedly thrive in a short-term program—thirty to ninety days. But thirty days is only the start. Making it to the finish requires more. A short-term program will provide limited effectiveness in preparing your loved one for lifelong sobriety and a drug-free life. These programs have the best of intentions. They clean out the addict's body, but this fresh slate will make it possible for the addict to experience a cherished "first-time high" as soon as they are discharged.

Any heroin addict will tell you they spend their years of addiction looking to re-experience their first high. I was no different. The first high is the best high because after you've been using for a while, the body builds up a tolerance to the chemicals and you are no longer able to reach that original state of euphoria.

In my case, I would check into rehab to detox so I could start shooting up again with clean blood as soon as I hit the streets. I wanted to feel that first-high again. And I wasn't the only addict to do it. I learned this trick from another patient the first time I detoxed.

Here's the real danger: when a drug addict detoxes and then goes out and uses again, they often use the same amount of drug they were using just before they detoxed. This astronomically increases the probability of overdose. After tolerance has been flushed out of an addict's system, the amount they used before rehab is too much for the body to handle after detox. When they haven't dealt with the mental, emotional, and spiritual parts of themselves, they are more susceptible to relapse, which sets them up for disaster. Even death.

Alcoholics face a different type of danger. While alcohol doesn't hold the same dangers of overdose after a period of sobriety as drugs do, an alcoholic still faces the likelihood of relapse and death. A slow expiration from cirrhosis of the liver, or other organ failures, may take longer, but is still torturous and destructive for all who are touched by it. Some say alcoholics are at greater risk because drinking is a legal and acceptable norm in our society.

An alcoholic can't go to dinner party or the grocery store without facing temptation and triggers. If your loved one abuses alcohol and chooses to do a stint at a short-term facility, they will barely touch the surface of what they need in order to live a sober and successful life. Sad to say, but most soon have one drink, which turns into two, and which turns into too many. Short-term solutions will send you back to this book, trying to figure out where it went wrong. There is no quick and easy fix when it comes to lifelong freedom from addiction.

Your loved one didn't get into this mess overnight, and they're not going to get out of it in a month. There is not enough time in a thirty-day program to get to the root problem. They must learn new life skills. A short-term program offers limited hope for lasting change and comes with its own consequences.

YOUR LOVED ONE DIDN'T GET INTO THIS MESS OVERNIGHT, AND THEY'RE NOT GOING TO GET OUT OF IT IN A MONTH. THERE IS NOT ENOUGH TIME IN A THIRTY-DAY PROGRAM TO GET TO THE ROOT PROBLEM. THEY MUST LEARN NEW LIFE SKILLS.

Many times, a short-term program provides your loved one with a new network of fellow addicts and dealers, all looking for access. These folks will be happy to put a lethal dose into your loved one's clean system once they're back on the street. Let's not ignore the fact that alcohol is readily available; no dealer is needed.

Most addicts who get through a short-term program transition to a halfway house. There are numerous reasons many do not make it beyond that. Right program, wrong time. Right program, wrong person. Right time, wrong program. You get the picture. You need the right program, at the right time when your loved one is ready. In reality, most addicts are ready for the change in stages.

For this reason, I designed New Life For Youth as a twelve-month program, with an optional six-month internship after graduation. This might sound like a long time, but it isn't. In fact, twelve to eighteen months is only the beginning. It doesn't take any time at all to detox a person. That's the simple part of the process. Getting a substance out of a person's body takes a lot less time than it does to replace it with good character, healthy coping skills, and preparation for a rewarding life. Quitting can happen quickly. But quitting doesn't stop the drug and alcohol habit. Healthy habits are only the *beginning* of what makes the difference. Continuing the process is where the real work is. And it takes time.

A long-term program gives your loved one the chance to progress through the various levels of surrender required for real change to take place. This is where they will learn to build a new life apart from drugs and alcohol—a lasting life of freedom.

Addiction creates a lifestyle, a culture that destroys the good character instilled in a person by his or her community. It replaces the value system of their youth with selfish, destructive behaviors. The lifestyle of addiction is composed of a lack of loyalty, poor work habits, irresponsibility, and lack of accountability—traits that poison a person's character.

We can feel confused when looking at our loved one. It's like looking at a stranger. The behavior doesn't fall in line with the value system they were taught. The reason you barely recognize them is because addiction has warped their character. But there is hope. They can be made new, just like it says in 2 Corinthians 5:17: *"Therefore if any man be in Christ, he is a new creature: old things are passed away; behold, all things are become new."* Character can be restored and replaced.

A long-term, residential treatment program that deals with the whole person can help to heal that character. But an exchange is required. Positive for negative. Healthy for unhealthy. If you have a full glass of water and all you do is pour it out, you're left with an empty glass. Sure, the water's gone, but nothing else is there.

Poor character falls away as good character is built. They can't co-exist. We want our loved ones to have a good life, and a good life grows out of good character. Matthew 7:18 illustrates it this way: *"A good tree cannot bring forth evil fruit, neither can a corrupt tree bring forth good fruit"* (Matthew 7:18). You want a program equipped to help your loved one develop good character.

3. How are they prepared for the next stage of their life?

Ask the program representative what they offer in the way of education, vocational training, life skills instruction, and career preparation. If the addict has children, ask about parenting classes. Many addicts are lacking in basic life skills, much less any sort of job experience or the ability to raise a child. You want them to have those things when they are released back into the world. A twelve-month program is better equipped to offer these services than shorter programs.

A lot of addicts never finished high school, another thing addiction stole from them. Ask you prospective treatment facility if they offer GED preparation so they can continue their education, if that is their dream.

Find out if the programs have job skills training. At New Life For Youth, our students take vocational classes throughout their program and get on-the-job mentoring in different areas to prepare them for the job market and a career. A time will come when your loved one's attention shifts from past to future.

COMMUNICATION, PROBLEM-SOLVING SKILLS, HANDLING EMOTIONS, SENSE OF SELF, RELATIONSHIPS, SPIRITUAL MATURITY, CONFLICT RESOLUTION, SELF-DISCIPLINE, GOAL-SETTING, SELFLESSNESS—ALL THESE SKILLS AND MORE ARE IMPACTED BY ADDICTION. THIS IS WHY THE TREATMENT CENTER YOU CHOOSE NEEDS TO ADDRESS AND EDUCATE IN THESE AREAS. IT'S NOT ENOUGH TO JUST TACKLE THE ADDICTION.

Your loved one will need guidance in deciding what they would like to do next. At New Life For Youth, in the last three or four months of their program or internship, we place them under the supervision of our exit coordinator, who takes them through the process of writing resumes, conducting job searches, interview preparation, and how to dress for the workplace. These are skills that a former addict or alcoholic may not have developed because of their vices. Your loved one, in spite of your best efforts to guide them, missed a lot in the way of basic life skills. Addiction had all their attention.

You might look at some of what we offer and think, *Well, that's just common sense.* But you would have missed a subliminal truth.

With addiction, there is no such thing as common sense. What we call common sense is really learned sense; it's experienced sense. And everyone's experience is different. Addicts come from all walks of life, and some are more equipped for life than others. The program you choose should prime them to thrive.

We say that a person's growth and maturity stop at the point in their life when the addiction starts. Communication, problem-solving skills, handling emotions, sense of self, relationships, spiritual maturity, conflict resolution, self-discipline, goal-setting, selflessness—all these skills and more are impacted by addiction. This is why the treatment center you choose needs to address and educate in these areas. It's not enough to just tackle the addiction.

4. Do they offer programs and support for the rest of the family?

Because addiction is a family problem and has devastated every member of the household, the entire family needs support. Yes, you want to get guidance on how to help your addicted loved one, but you need healing too. And so do other members of your household.

Whether you acknowledge it or not, this process has taken a toll on you. Having other people in your corner who have gone through what you're dealing with isn't just a recommendation, it is a necessity. Family support is vital in the recovery of your loved one, and in your own healing process as well. When you're researching recovery programs, inquire about what types of family support are offered.

5. How is the addict prepared for the next stage of their life?

What happens the day treament is over? Aftercare is a crucial aspect of any recovery program. Find out if this essential element for accountability and support is provided after your loved one has completed treatment. If treatment is local, your loved one needs face-to-face meetings. If they live far from the facility, they need access to regular support via telephone, online video calls, or even social media.

Speaking of social media, keep an eye on your loved one's social media habits. It can often be the first indicator a former student is making unhealthy decisions. Our loved ones may not tell us what's really going on, but if they go to unhealthy places, where will the proof be? That's right—social media.

6. What is the re-entry policy?

What if your loved one graduates, and then, down the road, stops doing the basics necessary for successful recovery? I'd love to say that 100 percent of the students who go through New Life For Youth stay clean and sober for the rest of their lives. But lifelong change is ultimately up to the individual. They have a free will.

Former students can make bad decisions and end up needing help again. While every program's guidelines vary, we have found it effective to allow former students re-entry for restoration purposes. Eligibility is decided on a case-by-case basis. Re-entry into the program is not guaranteed. The same goes for students who drop out of the program.

For any program, you and your loved one need to understand that re-entry is not guaranteed when they leave treatment. Their mental commitment is pivotal to their success. From the outset, they must tell themselves, *This is it. I've got to give this everything. I must surrender. I've run out of chances.*

If your loved one is not completely surrendered to the program, if they feel like they can quit and come back later on down the road, they are less likely to overcome their addiction. For some addicts, there won't be a "later on down the road." We have had to bury far too many young men and women because they left treatment before it was time. They never got another chance at freedom. Victory comes when they are ready, all in, and fully committed the first time they cross the threshold of a treatment program.

There are cases in which people don't quite get it the first time around and need another shot. Sometimes it takes repetition. But every delay contains risk.

ONCE YOU'VE CHOSEN A PROGRAM

For best results, your loved one should enter treatment ready to see it through to the end. This is about setting them up for success by not giving them a way out. Set high standards and get tough. If recovery isn't uncomfortable, your loved one isn't doing it right. Change is hard. There will be times when they want to leave. There may be times when they ask you to pick them up. That's okay. They can want to leave and they can ask you to help them leave. But you can't do it!

Brace and mentally prepare yourself for that conversation. They will come up with any excuse and sad story to convince you that they don't need to be in treatment anymore. Unbelievable excuses are the norm in this phase. Do your best to address every comment concerning their desire to leave with an encouraging and positive answer. Stand your ground, but listen. Then, calmly reaffirm why they are there and emphasize the goal.

In our program, students who are eligible get a day pass after three months. By that time, students feel better physically, have more energy, aren't thinking about getting high all the time, and exhibit confidence. Some will feel so confident, they think, *Okay. I've got this. I see how this is done. I'm fixed now. I don't need nine more months of this.* But one success is not enough.

Here's what they may do on that first pass. They try to get Mom and Dad, wife or husband, grandparent or friend, to see how great they're doing and let them drop out. If that doesn't work, they may try to convince you this program is too tough—after all, they weren't prepared for such introspection. If that doesn't get you to pull them out early, they may try to turn you against the staff or the program itself. I've heard every excuse in the book.

One student said, "It's too much work here."

Another told his atheist dad, "I knew it was a faith-based program, but I didn't realize there would be so much talk about faith."

Men and women in our program who have children use their parental responsibilities as a reason to leave treatment early. We hear statements like these:

"I need to be home for my kids."

"I need to go back home and get a job to provide for my family."

"It isn't fair for my parents to have to watch my kids."

I have to give it to them straight: "Man, you haven't worked in six years!" or "Your parents have had custody of your child since she was born four years ago. Really? What's another six months?"

Be ready, because your loved one will appeal to reason and tug on your emotions. Don't give in. You have to be ready with that *truth love* we talked about. No matter how pathetic your little girl sounds on the phone, to save her life, you have to say, "I hear how hard it is, but I'm not going to help you ruin your life. You're just going to have to stick with it."

It's also important that you know the rules and guidelines of the program. If you have questions about how things are done day-to-day, ask. You want to be ready with an answer and not be caught off guard if your loved one tries to pull one over on you. This is not so you can oppose them, but so you can encourage them. You worked and prayed so hard to get them into treatment. Now you have to work and pray to *keep* them in treatment.

By being proactive, you will be ready for whatever your loved one throws at you in a desperate attempt to get away from the pain of changing. Hold your ground. Transformation is happening. If it weren't, your loved one wouldn't be so uncomfortable. This is a good sign.

A WIFE'S STORY

Trying to find a place for my husband was almost as challenging as getting him to agree to receive help. I waited for the call from the police that he was dead. I almost lost him to the abuse of illegal substances several times. As a wife, I felt frustrated, hurt, and emotionally drained. I promised myself that if he didn't get help soon, I was going to leave.

Raising three children and trying to shield them from so much trauma was another feat. Throughout the years, we had exhausted many resources and we didn't know where to turn. He had been through quick detox programs and thirty-day programs. It seemed he'd do well for a week, sometimes a couple months. Our lives were a virtual roller coaster until someone told us about New Life For Youth.

At first, we didn't think we could commit to a year-long program. Without his income, I knew the financial stress would be overwhelming. On the other hand, burying my husband and raising three children alone would be devastating. We decided his life, our lives, were worth the twelve-month sacrifice.

Throughout that year, my husband was mentored. Their efforts poured into his life, and I began to see him change. As the months passed, his character transformed. Even with the obvious changes, I have to be honest, it took a while for me to trust him again. But something began happening inside of me, too.

I started attending the church the program students went to and began to grow. The Lord changed our hearts. His *and* mine. We grew spiritually, but also in very practical ways.

One of the things I appreciated the most was the vocational training my husband received in the program. He was always a hard worker—when he was employed. But without a specific skill, we could never quite make ends meet, even with my salary. He would get frustrated and end up fired or quitting.

At New Life For Youth, he was able to work with the program staff to learn carpentry, flooring, and HVAC. After graduation, he already had a job with a Christian company that builds new homes.

Getting him off drugs was one thing, but preparing him for a future was something he never received at any other rehab. I finally got my husband back, the kids got their dad back, and, together, we are building a new future.

A lot of prep and practice went into this man's treatment and final release, including follow-up mentoring.

Consistency between your home and the program is vital for stability and security. Everyone has to know your loved one is safe from temptation on those release passes. Keep in mind that your role isn't just to enforce the do's and don'ts, the rules and regulations. You also need to offer consistent, tender, loving responses tempered with grace and space.

Visits, as well as day and weekend passes, give you a chance to practice relating to each other as you're all healing. The program staff should prepare you, follow-up afterward with encouragement, and help with any issues. It's important to take a proactive approach by making your time together a healthy and positive experience. Going through treatment can feel overwhelming, so if your loved one gets moody, don't take it personally. Just keep encouraging.

By the time your loved one has their first opportunity to leave the grounds, you will have educated yourself on what the program expects and why. You'll be familiar with their day-to-day routines, and you'll be prepared to minister to your loved one in a positive way, as well as support them by following their new structured normal. What will your lives look like when they finish their program and come home? Let's explore that in the next chapter.

NEW LIFE SUCCESS STEPS

+ Do your homework. Google "treatment programs," but look beyond the home page. What are they about? What are their foundational beliefs? Are there endorsements from former participants and their families? Do they have a long track record of success? Have you verified their advertising claims?

+ Ensure the programs you consider cover the physical, emotional, mental, and spiritual aspects of addiction. Do they dig down to the root issues?

+ Are there online reviews or chats you can read through?

+ Check the Better Business Bureau to see if there are any claims against agencies you are considering.

+ Ask for references from those who've experienced their program, including contact information, so you can speak to some of them personally.

+ Consider the full scope of what a program has to offer. How do they prepare students for re-entry? What are their day-to-day routines? How do they equip graduates for successful, addiction-free living when they go back into the real world?

13

WHAT SHOULD I EXPECT WHEN MY LOVED ONE COMES OUT OF TREATMENT?

"I want to be remembered for my recovery, not my addiction."
—John

The long anticipated moment is finally here. It's a milestone. Your loved one is coming home. However, along with the anticipation comes a certain level of understandable anxiety. Your nerves may be getting to you. You may have felt more relaxed when your loved one was safe in rehab. The uncertainty of them coming home and reentering the big bad world has you biting your nails. But it's also brought you an opportunity for a higher level of faith.

Keep in mind, this is just the beginning, regardless of their time in treatment. Your loved one isn't "fixed." The treatment program you selected laid the groundwork and equipped your loved one with tools designed to help them live without substances. But they'll need to hone their coping and life skills to grow into the person they were created to be.

The human brain is complex. We can't flip a switch and have everything go back to the way it was before the addiction. In fact, it shouldn't go back to the way it was before; otherwise, the emptiness that drove your loved one to addiction will consume them again. Victory requires a change in our thoughts.

Transforming old thinking patterns is a process, a continual correction of poor mental habits, an intentional shift in what we allow to play in our minds. Romans 12:2 says, *"And be not conformed to this world: but be you transformed by the renewing of your mind, that you may prove what is that good, and acceptable, and perfect, will of God."* This transformation requires an active awareness of what messages your loved one allows themselves to receive and dwell on.

Supporting your loved one's healing when they come home will require your attention to mental messages. Even if you see some things that remind you of the old addict, let me encourage you: that person is gone. In the eyes of God, that person has been transformed. Watch that you don't react in old ways to this new person.

When we learn to view our loved one through two lenses, regeneration and transformation, the picture becomes clearer. *Regeneration* means "to generate again." Not a one-time starting over, but a constant and consistent process of internal rebirth.

During my regeneration process, I had the opportunity to go back to my old neighborhood, where I faced temptation, even though I had just walked out of rehab. I felt confident and strong. But as I neared my old hangouts, waves of panic washed over me. I became aware of the possibility that I would encounter drugs while I was there. Because God had made me new, and I was filled with the Holy Spirit, I had a feeling in my soul that reminded me of how much I had changed. Regeneration is beneath the surface, and it empowers the outward transformation.

The other lens, the transformation process, is the outward evidence of the new life of your loved one. If we stay connected to Christ and seek growth, transformation will be lifelong.

I have found that when a student surrenders to the process and does the work, they continue to flourish and figure out how to grow in their new reality. They are still learning. This is also *your* new reality. Everyone involved is learning how to navigate in this new, calmer, safer, healthier way of living. In the beginning, it often feels awkward to not worry or give them negative attention, like you used to when they were using or drinking.

IT IS INSTINCTIVE FOR US TO WANT TO HELP, BUT AFTER TREATMENT GRADUATION, WE HAVE TO BELIEVE IN THEIR ABILITY TO MAKE BETTER CHOICES FOR THEIR OWN LIFE. WE CAN WATCH, BUT WE MUSTN'T SMOTHER. WE CAN GUIDE, BUT WE SHOULD NOT ATTEMPT TO CONTROL. WE CAN LOVE, BUT LOVE SOMETIMES MEANS LETTING GO.

It is instinctive for us to want to help, but after treatment graduation, we have to believe in their ability to make better choices for their own life. We can watch, but we mustn't smother. We can guide, but we should not attempt to control. We can love, but love sometimes means letting go. You will have to resist the natural urge to micromanage every minute of their waking hours. Even though your motive is to protect, it could backfire and push them away.

WRITING A POST-TREATMENT AGREEMENT

Your loved one has likely come out of a program with a lot of rules. It's a good idea to write up an after-treatment agreement *together*. And it must work for everyone involved. Expectations set too low can leave your loved one unprotected, which can lead to trouble. If the rules are too rigid, your loved one can feel that they have no say in their own life, throwing them into rebellion.

I wish I could be more specific on what your agreement should say, but every family is different. What works for one might not work for another. How much of your involvement is too much is something you will have to figure out as a family, working *together*. While I can't tell you every detail that your family's after-treatment agreement should contain, I do provide a sample as a template or guide in the resource section.

I strongly urge you to have a written and signed agreement with your loved one in place prior to their leaving the program. Do not hesitate. Do not wait. Do it *before* they come home. This is especially important if they will be living in your home.

A written agreement outlines the expectations and needs of all family members as you move forward to a place of peace and healing. Once you review the sample agreement I provide, decide how to personalize it. If something doesn't work, make adjustments.

A word of caution: do not chisel your family's after-treatment agreement in stone. Be open to making changes as your family transforms through this process. If what used to work doesn't anymore, that's okay. Alter it as needed. Be patient with your loved one, other family members, and yourself in the process, as you learn to communicate and interact with each other in healthy ways. None of you are the same as you were before addiction came into the picture. The whole family has been hurt and needs time to heal. If you choose a program with strong family support and take advantage of what is offered, more than likely, you're already healing and improving communication.

Be on guard against old patterns of behavior and ways of communicating that won't work anymore. Maybe they never did. There is a danger of slipping back into those time-worn patterns if you're not being intentional and aware. This doesn't just apply to the one with the addiction history. This applies to everyone involved.

I think about the terrible things I did when I was a heroin addict and all the gang violence I was involved in. I robbed people. I stole from my family. As a young teenager, I even stabbed a guy. God forgave me. My parents forgave me. I also had to learn how to forgive myself.

I know how far addiction can take us and how many people can be taken down with us. Even though our addicted loved one is not the same person who entered treatment, sometimes people cannot bring themselves to forgive past offenses. Your loved one will have to face the people they have hurt. It is necessary to seek restitution and peace. Romans 12:18 says, *"If it be possible, as much as lies in you, live peaceably with all men."* This can be difficult and intimidating.

But what if the damage is too great? you wonder. Forgiveness takes time. There's usually at least one family member who has difficulty letting go of wrongs committed against them. It's not easy to release pain, so be mindful of that. In your loved one's addiction, they may have done something so horrible, so devastating, that unless God steps in, forgiveness will never come from the person on the receiving end. Some of those relationships will be put right, but some won't. The aftermath is part of this battle. Your loved one will have to live with that.

The Bible says, in Matthew 6:14, *"If you forgive men their trespasses, your heavenly Father will also forgive you."* When an addicted loved one comes home, patience, grace, and love need to flow in abundance from all directions. If they went to a faith-based program, then they learned their sins have been erased. Your loved one may have the hardest time forgiving themselves. But God has forgiven them. Your loved one need not be crushed by the guilt of past wrongs.

POST-TREATMENT LIFE AT HOME

In the previous chapter, I shared practical ways to find the right treatment program for your loved one. Now it's time to bring the treatment home. The first time back in the real world is a testing ground for an addicted loved one—and you. Odds are, both of you will ask yourselves these kinds of questions:

- How will they handle themselves without program staff around?

- Will they still follow the rules?

- Can you truly restore your relationship?

- Will other family members and friends accept the transformed person who came home?

- Will the compulsion to drink or use overtake them again?

These are scary questions, and there are no guarantees. But there are a few more preparations you need to make before your loved one walks through the door. Once they've arrived home, there are physical actions that should be done together. These steps will give your family and your loved one a greater chance of achieving permanent change.

Prepare the environment.

If you have alcohol in the house, get rid of it. Maybe the other drinkers in the house don't have an addiction, but your loved one does. And if the other drinkers in the house don't have an addiction, then they shouldn't have an issue with clearing the house of all substances. I have to be direct here. Your loved one's life is at stake.

Safeguard any prescription medications.

Be aware that alcohol-based hand sanitizers, mouthwash, and even baking products like vanilla extract can be a temptation. You think I'm kidding? I've seen it. A desperate addict drinking hand sanitizer sounds ridiculous, but it's not as uncommon as you think. Protect your loved one at the risk of seeming over-the-top.

If you didn't do it during treatment, clean out their contact list.

Cell phone, Facebook, and other social media accounts are often full of unhealthy contacts from dangerous relationships. This is huge and not an easy step for your loved one. Cutting off ties is hard but necessary. Support them while they completely delete old social media accounts and create new profiles that represent the transformed person they've become. This will set them up to make healthy, new contacts. If they hesitate in deleting any contacts, encourage them to figure out *why*.

CELL PHONE, FACEBOOK, AND OTHER SOCIAL MEDIA ACCOUNTS ARE OFTEN FULL OF UNHEALTHY CONTACTS FROM DANGEROUS RELATIONSHIPS. THIS IS HUGE AND NOT AN EASY STEP FOR YOUR LOVED ONE. CUTTING OFF TIES IS HARD BUT NECESSARY. SUPPORT THEM WHILE THEY COMPLETELY DELETE OLD SOCIAL MEDIA ACCOUNTS AND CREATE NEW PROFILES THAT REPRESENT THE TRANSFORMED PERSON THEY'VE BECOME.

Search their room and car for hidden substances or paraphernalia.

You would be surprised where addicts stash drugs. They honestly may not remember they have a bag of dope taped under their sock drawer. They might have forgotten they put pills inside a Zippo lighter. But at some point, that memory will pop back in their heads. The enemy will make sure of it. Addiction is sneaky. If you aren't sure where to look or what to look for, ask your loved one if you can get a more experienced friend to help you with the project.

Be respectful and remind your loved one that you are setting them up for success. If you *do* find something stashed away, don't assume they knew it was there all along. They may have been high when they hid it and really don't remember. Keep in mind that it was put there by that old addict, not the new creation that came home to you. No judgment.

Guard against people, places, and things.

This is one of the basics. Your loved one needs to take proactive steps to avoid old party friends, any place that has a drug memory, or things, including but not limited to, music, movies, and television shows that were part of their old life or have drug-related themes. All need to go, most of them permanently. The thought of living without can throw them into panic. But it's always better to remove temptation than take a chance on relapse.

If you chose the right treatment program, your loved one stuck it out, you've created a solid agreement, chosen grace, mercy, and forgiveness, and everyone is committed to following what has been agreed to, the odds of success escalate. Your loved one can come home and contribute to a new, more peaceful existence.

But what if your loved one never made it to treatment? Or what if they've been in one a dozen times with no real change? Is there a time to throw your hands up in utter defeat? In the next chapter, we'll discuss how to handle your addicted loved one when it seems all has failed. You are not the first to face this valid concern.

NEW LIFE SUCCESS STEPS

+ Prepare, sign, and follow an after-treatment agreement with your loved one. When we put things in writing, our minds pay closer attention. It's harder to break your word when you've etched it in a contract.

+ Support sustained healthy choices. Remove or lock up all alcohol and any drugs from your loved one's environment. Don't forget alcohol-based products like hand sanitizer or over-the-counter medications. Filter out unhealthy people, places, and things. Encourage structure and discipline, including peer groups like Celebrate Recovery, Narcotics Anonymous, and Alcoholics Anonymous, if the program your loved one came through doesn't offer their own.

+ Be proactive in avoiding conflict. Airing grievances as soon as possible will lessen the likelihood of negative thoughts and emotions damaging relationships.

+ Practice expressing your needs. Addiction is self-serving, so it may take your loved one time to learn to stop being the center of attention. You have likely been pushing your own needs and desires to the back burner, so this may take some getting used to for you, as well.

+ Be flexible. Whether today was a good day, or a difficult one, tomorrow may bring a completely opposite experience. Guide what you can; the rest goes to God to handle.

+ Be patient. Consistency will come—maybe not today, perhaps you won't see it tomorrow, either. But keep doing the next right thing and making the healthy choices and one day, peace will be the norm for your family.

+ Believe that.

14

WHEN SHOULD I GIVE UP ON MY LOVED ONE?

"You mustn't confuse a single failure with a final defeat."
—*F. Scott Fitzgerald*
Tender Is the Night

C an you relate to these feelings?

I'm just tired of it all.

I'm tired of the fighting.

I'm tired of hearing my family crying at night.

I'm tired of how the neighbors look at me after the police have come to my door at 3:00 AM, three nights in a row.

I'm tired of getting calls from the school, the job, the emergency room.

I'm tired of posting bail.

I'm tired of feeling like the people at church are talking about me.

I'm tired of feeling crazy.

I'm tired of my own guilt and fear.

I'm tired of feeling like I'm letting everyone else down.

I'm tired of wondering if the next time will be the fatal time.

I'm tired of panicking every time the phone rings.

I'm tired of the lies and the broken promises.

I'm tired of hoping.

I have nothing else to give.

I'm done.

I. Am. Done!

If that's how you're feeling right now, you're not alone. If you have never felt any of those things, you will if your loved one continues in their addiction. I'm sorry, but this is the truth.

Somewhere along the dark journey, each of us wants to give up and be done with it. If the addiction lasts for many years, you may feel this way more than once. Why? Because you are living in a nightmare. It's completely understandable to want out. Who wouldn't?

When facing your addicted loved one, you don't have to feel guilty for wishing you could throw your hands up and walk away. This is next to the hardest thing you will ever have to do. But it's not the hardest.

The hardest thing you might face is burying your loved one and wishing you hadn't given up. So don't. Don't give up. You are not wrong for feeling like throwing in the towel. It's okay to feel like it. Just don't do it.

When should you give up? The simple answer is: when they're dead, not a minute before. If there is breath, there is hope. This may sound harsh, but sometimes, we need a wake-up call to give us the stamina to continue.

We can't read our loved one's mind to know when they are just one event away from being tired of the way they've been living. We can't see what's around the corner, that one thing that turns them around and makes them recognize they need help.

"IF I COULD HAVE SEEN LAND, I KNOW I COULD HAVE MADE IT."

In a strange way, the example of Florence Chadwick motivates me to keep pushing forward. Maybe you've heard it.

A long-distance, open-water swimmer, Florence set a time record and was the first woman to swim the English Channel both ways. She started setting records when she was ten years old. But this story isn't about her successes. This is about her failure.

In the early 1950s, Florence was thirty-four years old when she attempted to swim the Catalina Channel[24]: twenty-one miles of choppy water between Catalina Island and the California coast.[25] Florence swam with small boats on each side of her. Her support crew occasionally shot into the water to keep sharks away. They were also there in case she got injured. One of the support boats carried her trainer and her mother, both of whom encouraged her along the way.

After Florence swam for about fifteen hours—can you imagine that?—the weather changed. The temperature dropped. The water turned bitterly cold. A dense fog rolled in. Even with boats surrounding her and her mom's encouragement, Florence became disoriented and didn't think she could make it all the way. She stuck it out for another hour, but her mind had already given up.

Finally, at her urging, the crew from one of the support boats pulled her out of the water. As she sat in the boat, Florence learned she had

---

24. Susan Ware and Stacy Braukman (editors), *Notable American Women: A Biographical Dictionary Completing the Twentieth Century* (Cambridge, MA: Radcliffe Institute for Advanced Study, Harvard University, 2004).
25. See also http://wwwqueenofthechannel.com/florence-chadwick, and the book *Remarkable Women of San Diego: Pioneers, Visionaries and Innovators* by Hannah S. Cohen and Gloria G. Harris.

stopped swimming one-half mile away from her goal. On July 4, 1952, Independence Day, after being in the water for almost sixteen hours, Florence gave up fifteen minutes from shore. When Florence was interviewed about the disappointing event, she told a reporter, "Look, I'm not excusing myself, but if I could have seen land, I know I could have made it."

Like Florence, we don't know what lies ahead, just within our reach.

Your loved one's behavior, your family's circumstances, your own pain and exhaustion are understandable reasons to give up and climb into the boat. We're all human. We are surrounded by the fog of our human shortsightedness. If you give up today, however, you could be quitting on what would have been you and your loved one's Independence Day. Don't give up before your loved one chooses freedom over the chains of addiction and changes their story forever.

Because she couldn't see anything, Florence must have felt like she was swimming in place and going nowhere. Is that how you feel sometimes? Like you're getting nowhere? For more encouragement, here's the rest of the story.

Florence gave up that day, but she didn't completely give up. She went back to the Catalina Channel and tried again, this time with a successful outcome. She did it in thirteen hours and forty-seven minutes, breaking a twenty-seven-year-old record by more than two hours.

Was the second attempt held on a warm, sunny day? No. The weather turned on her on that day, too. The fog rolled in just as it did the first time. It was so dense she couldn't see anything around her, just as it was the day she gave up. Only this time, she didn't quit.

How did she keep going the second time in the same conditions that made her quit the first time? When asked, she said she kept a mental image of the shoreline in her mind while she swam. Keeping her eye on the prize kept her going.

In Proverbs 29:18, the Bible says, "*Where there is no vision, the people perish.*" We have to do what Florence did. When there are no signs that our goal is within reach, we have to keep a picture of it in our minds. You can't see daylight right now, and maybe you have longer than a half-mile left before you touch the shore. Even so, don't give up.

The powerful lesson in this amazing story is that Florence didn't fail the first time because the task was impossible. She failed because she quit.

Giving up is the catalyst for defeat. Christians often say, "Give it to God." Taking your hands off and giving it to God is not the same as giving up. Putting our loved ones in God's hands means we understand we are not the heart-changers. We don't have the power to transform a person from the inside out. As I said in chapter 3, sometimes you need to realize that not all of your helping is actually helping.

GIVING UP IS THE CATALYST FOR DEFEAT. CHRISTIANS OFTEN SAY, "GIVE IT TO GOD." TAKING YOUR HANDS OFF AND GIVING IT TO GOD IS NOT THE SAME AS GIVING UP. PUTTING OUR LOVED ONES IN GOD'S HANDS MEANS WE UNDERSTAND WE ARE NOT THE HEART-CHANGERS. WE DON'T HAVE THE POWER TO TRANSFORM A PERSON FROM THE INSIDE OUT.

You have accepted that there are areas in which you need to step away so God can deal with your loved one in whatever way He sees fit. That isn't quitting or giving up hope. It's giving them to God, who *is* our Hope.

Parents, sisters, brothers, grandparents, aunts, uncles, friends, cousins, and coworkers have seen their prayers answered because they believed the vision in their minds before they actually saw their loved one set free. They were courageous enough to trust God to do what only He could.

"YOU WILL NOT DIE"

Carl's grandmother fits that description. For over two decades, she fought for the life of her grandson. When the rest of the family gave up, including his own mother, Carl's grandmother gave it to God. He told me this powerful story.

> Me-maw never quit on me through twenty-two long years. I dropped out of school, was in and out of jail, and was nobody anyone wanted to be around. I was mean. I wasn't a good guy. But my grandmother didn't see that. I mean, she saw it. She wasn't blind to how I was living, even though I tried to hide it. But she saw something else deep inside of me.
>
> Everybody thought that woman was crazy for believing in me. They told her to forget about me, that I was never going to change. I even told her to get on with her life and pretend I was dead. I figured it wouldn't be long before that was true. But she told me, "Carl, I don't listen to people. I listen to God. One day you will, too. You will not die."
>
> Eventually, I was in a bad car wreck that killed my girlfriend. We were both drunk and she was driving. I was in the hospital for over a month. Nobody came to see me except Me-maw. You know, that's a lonesome place to be. Nobody cared if I was alive or dead. I didn't either.
>
> Me-maw's own health was going downhill, but she sat there beside my bed and read the Bible to me, even when I was unconscious. When I woke up and got clear-headed, she said, "See, Carl? I told you, you wasn't gonna die."
>
> I can't say everything changed right then, but I started to believe that maybe I did have a life ahead of me, one that, up until then, only Me-maw could see. That belief started my change.
>
> I have been sober for seven years. My grandmother lived to see me become the person she knew I could be. I'm sure she had her

moments of doubt in those twenty-two years, but both she and her God were stronger than any demon of alcoholism.

Carl's grandmother kept her eye on the prize. She envisioned the shore before she got there.

Parenting is not for wimps. Marriage is not for cowards. Relationships require work. Life is hard, even if no substance abuse is in the picture. Nobody is saying any of this is easy. Your loved one might have hurt you so deeply, you don't know how you will ever forgive him. Addiction is messy. Life is messy.

But if you've gotten this far and are reading this chapter, that tells me you aren't giving up and walking away, even if you feel like it. You are looking for a reason to hold on, to fight another day. Let me give you that reason.

The Bible says God created you for a purpose. He also made your loved one with a purpose. Jeremiah 29:11 confirms it: *"For I know the plans I have for you, declares the Lord, plans for welfare and not for evil, to give you a future and a hope"* (ESV).

We didn't accidentally show up one day, forcing God to come up with something for us to do. No. It's the other way around. There are voids in the world, and God picks us to fill specific voids. You and your addicted loved one are included in His good plans, even when it seems like your loved one is making life a nightmare for you.

THERE ARE VOIDS IN THE WORLD, AND GOD PICKS US TO FILL SPECIFIC VOIDS. YOU AND YOUR ADDICTED LOVED ONE ARE INCLUDED IN HIS GOOD PLANS, EVEN WHEN IT SEEMS LIKE YOUR LOVED ONE IS MAKING LIFE A NIGHTMARE FOR YOU.

Your loved one was born because God has a plan for him or her. The enemy will try anything he can to distort that purpose. Addiction is one of his lethal weapons. But your loved one isn't thinking about their purpose right now. Their life goal right now is to escape reality. They can't see the sharks circling and the fog clouding their view. It's up to us to keep that picture of a healthy future in mind, as Carl's grandmother did. When they can't, or won't, do it for themselves, we still encourage them to envision the shore. You may not know what their shore will look like, but you *can* be sure there is a God-given destiny for your loved one.

My favorite verse is 1 Corinthians 2:9: *"Eye has not seen, nor ear heard, neither have entered into the heart of man, the things which God has prepared for them that love Him."*

I was a heroin addict and a member of a violent street gang. Do you think I ever could have pictured myself writing a book to help people get *off* drugs? But my mother knew God had something great waiting on the shore beyond addiction. She knew I had a future beyond how I was living.

I'm telling you, I would not be here if my parents had given up on me. But my mom kept praying and got other people to pray with her. For seven years, despite how bleak it looked on the outside, she believed and prayed. She wasn't messing around. No enemy was going to take her son.

My mother had a vision of what I could become. She kept that picture of me in her heart even when I walked out and slammed the door in her face. She saw me serving God, even when I was arrested. I told her she was crazy, but she clung to the belief that, one day, I would be free. When I overdosed, she rocked my limp body in her arms and refused to give up. She screamed at an invisible enemy and told him he could not have me. She paced the floor of our little apartment and claimed a future for my life, when it looked as though I wouldn't live long enough to have a future.

She kept on because she knew I was made for more than the needle. She told God she believed it. She screamed it at the devil. She told my family and anyone who would listen. She took my skin-and-bones face in her hands when I could barely hold my head up, and said, "Victor, you are made for more than this."

Your loved one was made for more than this. Don't give up. Instead, dare to believe while you pray. Pray, pray, and then pray some more. And after that, pray. Have faith enough for both of you. Have faith enough for the whole family if you have to. But do not give up.

Keep on fighting for your addicted loved one until they can do battle for themselves. Is there still breath in their body? Then there is still hope.

Choose to believe beyond what you can see.

When should you give up? Never. Never, never, ever.

+ Ignore the fog.

+ Picture their future.

+ Believe the vision.

+ Cling to it.

+ And keep swimming for the shore.

In the next chapter, we're going to tackle one more rough subject: relapse. Is it a given? Can you protect them? If your loved one has been clean, but your worst fears happen, how do you and they survive?

NEW LIFE SUCCESS STEPS

+ Consistently speak words of hope and health to your loved one.

+ Don't allow current circumstances to dictate your future.

+ Search out and read motivational stories, quotes, and inspiring words to help you swim when you feel like getting out of the race before you reach the shore.

+ Surround yourself with "never-give-up" messages. Write them on Post-Its and place them in your car, on your refrigerator, on your bathroom mirror, or in your wallet. Anywhere you routinely look can offer spontaneous motivation when you need it most.

+ Talk to people whose loved ones have succeeded in overcoming addiction. Schedule time to listen to their stories. Odds are, they will understand exactly where you are emotionally and they will have words of wisdom to help you through.

15

HOW DO I PREPARE
FOR RELAPSE?

"Tomorrow hopes we have learned something from yesterday."
—*John Wayne*

If you've made it to the place on this journey where you are thinking about a relapse prevention plan, it probably means you are not dealing with active addiction anymore. That's good news.

Maybe your loved one is close to completing a treatment program. Maybe they're already home, and you're trying to keep them safe. Maybe something has shifted, and you're seeing behaviors that concern you. You want to catch it before a wrong move becomes a slip, and a slip turns into a fall. Being proactive is key. You're on the right track.

There are many schools of thought regarding relapse. Some professionals believe relapse is a natural part of recovery and should be *expected*. Some say it's common and a recovered addict will *probably* have one or more relapses. Recovery does take practice. Living a life free from substance abuse requires rehearsal. It takes time.

That is why a short-term treatment facility is less effective than something long-term. Putting a newly clean person back into the world before they've had the chance to experience some of the different situations and emotions that can lead to relapse is setting them up for a fall. (Review the information in chapter 12 on selecting a treatment program.)

Here's the problem I see with *expecting* relapse. Coming out of treatment into a community that presumes and accepts relapse as a natural part of recovery weakens a person's determination to stay drug-free and sober. There's no point in giving any effort to recovery if everybody relapses. When we tell them relapse is expected, we are practically giving them permission to use or drink again. Do you see the challenge?

I do not believe relapse has to happen for everyone. I do not believe it's a necessary part of recovery. That line of thinking is based on the belief that once a person is an addict, they will always be an addict. Many still believe there is no cure for addiction. I am not one of those people.

In this chapter, you will notice I use the term *former addict* when I refer to a person who used to use drugs or drink but doesn't anymore. I know this flies in the face of the conventional approach to recovery, but here's why I believe this is an important distinction.

If you used to smoke three packs of cigarettes a day and quit smoking, do you still refer to yourself as a smoker? Of course not. If you quit smoking a year ago, do you still buy cigarettes? Carry a lighter? Sit in the smoking section? No. You avoid anything to do with smoking. So, why would we still call you a smoker? We wouldn't. Nobody says, "Once a smoker, always a smoker." If you don't smoke, you've quit.

In the same way, if a person doesn't do drugs or drink, even if they used to, they are not an addict. They used to be one. They could be again. But right now, they are clean.

I won't get too deep into this because I am not a medical professional, but the scientific community is discovering that the brain can recover from addiction. The brain's ability to adapt, change, and learn is called *neuroplasticity*. It's a fancy term that simply means the brain is moldable.

Marc Lewis is a neuroscientist and professor of developmental psychology. In his *Psychology Today* online article, "Recovery (like Addiction) Relies on Neuroplasticity," Dr. Lewis writes, "There's nothing chronic about this 'chronic brain disease'."[26]

He is telling us that the person you love who used to do drugs is not stuck in that prison for the rest of his or her life! Dr. Lewis is not only a scientist but a *former* addict as well. He experimented with a variety of drugs in his youth until he finally got hooked on opiates. It cost him relationships and landed him in trouble with the law. Sound familiar?

Lewis quit drugs for good when he was thirty, went back to grad school, and got his Ph.D. five years later. Soon afterward, he began his research. His studies as a neuroscientist led him to investigate brain changes that strengthen cravings and weaken self-control. Then he discovered the opposite is also true. The brain can revert, making cravings fewer and weaker and self-control stronger. He writes, "Neuroplasticity is the brain's natural starting point for all learning processes—processes that might include not only addiction but also recovery."[27] In other words, an addict can learn recovery the same way he or she learned addiction, through repetition over time.

Science has once again proven that God was right. In the Bible, there's a letter from the apostle Paul to the church in Rome. In Romans 12:2, he wrote, *"Be not conformed to this world: but be you transformed by the renewing of your mind, that you may prove what is that good, and acceptable, and perfect, will of God."* If it were impossible for the mind to change or be renewed, God wouldn't have told us it could be. So, what does this have to do with relapse? Relapse is not a given, but at the same time, recovery is not guaranteed. That's an important statement. Let's look closer at these two thoughts.

---

26. Marc Lewis Ph.D., "Recovery (like Addiction) Relies on Neuroplasticity," *Psychology Today*, December 7, 2015, https://www.psychologytoday.com/us/blog/addicted-brains/201512/recovery-addiction-relies-neuroplasticity (accessed September 13, 2018).
27. Ibid.

Galatians 5:1 breaks down both of these truths: *"It is for freedom that Christ has set us free. Stand firm, then, and do not let yourselves be burdened again by a yoke of slavery"* (NIV). I'll show you how this Scripture applies to addiction recovery and relapse.

RELAPSE IS NOT A GIVEN, BUT AT THE SAME TIME, RECOVERY IS NOT GUARANTEED.

---

1. RELAPSE IS NOT A GIVEN

In the first part of the verse, Paul wrote, *"It is for freedom that Christ has set us free."* We Christians like that part and quote it a lot. There's victory and freedom in Christ. That gets us excited because it's true. No matter what your beliefs are, I would not be helping you if I didn't tell you what I believe, what I know from my experience to be true. Deliverance through the love and power of Christ is a real thing. But we have to live it out.

A criminal who is released from prison doesn't walk around in his orange jumpsuit. He doesn't go to work in shackles. He's free. It's not a given that he will go back to prison. And your loved one doesn't have to go back to the chains of addiction. Freedom is possible through Jesus Christ. We can live in it for the rest of our lives, if we choose to. *If* we choose to. Relapse is not a given. And this brings us to our second statement and the second part of this verse.

2. RECOVERY IS NOT GUARANTEED

We don't hear as much about the second part of Galatians 5:1 because it requires something from us. It's the *Buy One* part of *Buy One, Get One*

Free. The last half of this verse is the instruction, the warning, the condition. If it's not heeded, that's when relapse happens.

We know we have been set free. But to continue walking in that freedom, we must *"Stand firm, then, and do not let yourselves be burdened again by a yoke of slavery."*

There it is. Your loved one *had* an addiction. They found freedom. It's up to them to not allow themselves to be burdened again by the yoke of slavery to drugs or alcohol. Even though we're not saying we expect a relapse, we do want to prepare by staying strong and walking in victory. Let me demonstrate.

My children, and then my grandchildren, loved fire drills at school (unless it was raining or they were at lunch). They liked getting out of class. The drill prepared the kids in case of an actual fire emergency. The boys and girls needed to know how to line up, single-file. They had to know which hallway to walk down and where the nearest exit was. They needed to know where to gather once they had made it outside safely. The school prepared for an emergency, even though they weren't expecting one.

That's what we're doing here. We're getting you prepared in case of emergency. Even with all your planning, preparation, and prayers, relapse can happen. It happens the same way addiction happened when it first started—through choices.

EVEN WITH ALL YOUR PLANNING, PREPARATION, AND PRAYERS, RELAPSE CAN HAPPEN. IT HAPPENS THE SAME WAY ADDICTION HAPPENED WHEN IT FIRST STARTED—THROUGH CHOICES.

The first wrong choice is never going to be the act of getting high or drinking. Relapse requires a setup. It's not an all-of-a-sudden decision to run out and get high or have some drinks. Relapse is sneakier and more subtle than that. It happens as the former addict starts making small allowances that let unhealthy behaviors sneak back in. This is where relapse gets an upgrade from possible to probable. Be aware of the dangers, stay in tune with what's going on in your loved one's life, and be prepared to respond to those early signs.

I'm not trying to scare you, but I am trying to prepare you. It's wise to be ready at all times for the moment of temptation, although we do not know the precise moment it will arrive. The Bible says, "*Wherefore let him that thinks he stands take heed lest he fall*" (1 Corinthians 10:12).

You are in a position of advantage because you are now educated and experienced. Helping to keep your loved one standing firm and focused on their goals is important. Here's a simple rule of thumb to follow: *what got you healthy will keep you healthy.*

If you notice any shift in your loved one's behavior, pay attention. Remember what I said in my introduction? We are the Navy SEALs of addiction. This book has equipped you with special training and preparation, with God's help, for battle, if necessary. One crucial aspect is recognizing the warning signs.

WARNING SIGNS

The following behaviors are signs of a set-up for relapse, or indications that relapse has already occurred. If you know what to look for, you can attack these shifts before they lead to further regression.

1. Glorifying the past—minimizing the devastating effects of addiction.

This is where it begins. The set-up for relapse starts in the mind and the heart; it sneaks in through thoughts. How do you know what your loved one is thinking? If you're listening, he or she will tell you. As the Bible says, the mouth speaks of what fills the heart. "*For of the abundance of the heart his mouth speaks*" (Luke 6:45).

If your loved one starts telling stories about past drug or alcohol use, parties, former friends, and the old life in a way that tries to make those times sound fun and adventurous, they are experiencing a thought-shift. Their mind is abandoning the true view of the devastation of their past addicted life. It's a set-up.

The enemy tries to turn their thinking back to the old way of seeing that lifestyle. The enemy wants to make that dangerous past seem acceptable and attractive again. Bring it to your loved one's attention. If the relapse set-up can be caught and stopped at the *thought* stage, it won't have a chance to become *action* and take your loved one to new levels of destruction.

2. Less prayer, Bible study, and church activities.

If your loved one went through a Christian treatment program, then prayer, Bible study, and church attendance have become a part of their new life. If that vital foundation weakens, the structure of their lives, including their sobriety, will collapse. It's like the old saying, "An idle mind is the devil's workshop." I believe the most powerful infusion of strength a former addict can get is to stay connected to a local church and a life filled with spiritual activities.

3. Less involvement in support groups, programs, or support systems.

Former addicts can get to the point where they think they've "got this." When that happens, they slowly stop doing the things that keep them healthy and on track. If your loved one finds one reason or another to miss going to a group or avoids spending time with their healthy support system, they might need reminders of the benefit of that type of back-up. This includes involvement in something that has a definite and clear purpose, such as volunteering and helping others.

4. Isolation.

Everyone needs time to themselves, but avoiding interaction with family and beneficial friendships can be a red flag. The sheep that gets separated from the flock gets eaten by the wolf.

5. Lack of routine.

Being in a healthy routine helps keep a former addict on track. When discipline and order begin to slip, other areas of life can get out of control. As with all these points, this can be a sign that relapse has already happened or is a sign that your loved one is not standing firm in avoiding the yoke of slavery, like we read in Galatians 5:1.

6. Other signs of addiction.

You know the signs. You've been there. Once relapse has happened, those signs we listed in chapter 1 will reappear. Loss of interest in normal activities, changes in appearance, time lapses, deception, manipulation, legal and health issues—all are possible indicators.

If your loved one shows signs of addiction again, here is what my mother would say if she were here to give you advice: "This thing is not over. You are not defeated. God still has a plan for your child, and you cannot quit now. I know you thought this was over, that you could finally breathe easy. But I also know you have the strength for another battle in you because God will fight for you. Don't give up."

If this is where you are, call your support system. Get your prayer warriors together like my mother did. In 2 Corinthians 4:9, the Word of God says, no matter what, we are *"cast down, but not destroyed."*

Get up and fight the good fight of faith. Don't blame yourself. You know the enemy will tell you it's your fault. He's tried that with you before. But now, you have the tools you need to help your loved one make the best possible choices. You are doing everything you can. Never forget, though, that their choices are theirs, not yours.

And it's *not* back to the drawing board. In some recovery programs, you *lose the clean time* and go back to day one. But this isn't logical or scriptural. How do you lose time? How do you unlearn what you've learned?

Let's say you are on the road with your family on vacation. You are driving along when, three hundred-sixty miles into a seven-hundred-mile trip, your car gets a flat tire. You pull the car over and wait for roadside assistance or a Good Samaritan to help fix your flat tire. Once the tire is fixed and you start the car, are you sent back to where you started? No! Those three hundred-sixty miles you've driven aren't erased just because you broke down. You aren't forced to start over like you've gone nowhere. You made it three hundred-sixty miles. They count for something. You continue the trip from the place of the breakdown. Relapse can follow the same concept.

Our loved one has grown. They've learned new behaviors, even if they messed up by choosing not to use the recovery tools they were given. We're not going to rob them of that. Their growth isn't undone by a relapse. The lessons they've learned don't fall out of their heads. God's grace gets them back on the road. Not only do they get back on track, but they continue their journey with a new tire.

NEW LESSONS WITH FRESH MOTIVATION

While writing this chapter, I took a break and walked downstairs to my kitchen. I had forgotten there were several young men at my house, all graduates of our New Life For Youth program. They were doing some work for me at my house. As we stood sipping warm coffee, one of them expressed his thankfulness for our ministry and how much he has learned. He shared his experience in another one-year program before coming to New Life. After completing that first treatment, he relapsed and went back to drugs.

He said, "My relapse taught me some great lessons. My biggest mistakes were when I separated myself from the people who loved and cared about me and when I stopped praying and reading my Bible."

Let this young man's real-world education encourage you. You made a commitment to your loved one, and you are seeing it through. If your loved one has relapsed, gather the strength to journey on, until you can welcome them back into your life, healed. Restoration is possible for both of you.

In our final chapter, we'll focus on taking our loved ones back—finally and fully. Lasting peace is possible, even after addiction.

NEW LIFE SUCCESS STEPS

+ Focus on the facts. The science of neuroplasticity proves the human brain can be trained and retrained. This is good news. Your loved one is not destined for relapse. But even if they do, they can draw from what they learned and get back on the recovery highway again.

+ Don't ignore warning signs. You've been taught what to look for and how to handle the truth. This knowledge provides wisdom you can apply if needed.

+ Don't assume. Relapse is not a given. Recovery is not guaranteed.

16

TAKING YOUR LOVED ONE BACK: FREEDOM, HEALING, AND ULTIMATE VICTORY FOR HURTING FAMILIES WOUNDED BY ADDICTION

"Don't give up on the people you love. Your patience and faithfulness
may be exactly what they need to make a complete turnaround."
—*Joyce Meyers*

This is the story of Mike, who had completed the twelve-month program at New Life Men's Ranch.

MIKE'S STORY

I've been restored. My mind is renewed and free from the substances that controlled it. The truth is, I was good at starting a lot of things, but this was the first time I ever finished something.

When they called my name during my program graduation, it felt like I had received a certificate from college. I broke down and my voice cracked a little when I looked out into the audience and saw both my parents. The last time I felt so valued and loved was when I played sports as a kid. It was hard to keep it together. They were both crying. They were so proud of me and grateful to God.

I really hurt them. You don't know the way I treated them. I think about that a lot. I never meant to, but addiction possessed me. I caused my entire family so much pain, worry, and heartache. But they never gave up fighting for my life. As I stood up there and spoke about my past experience and what I want for my future, I knew the completion certificate I got was theirs, too.

You don't know what it's like, to be helpless to do what you want to do, powerless to stop doing what you know is killing you. The only option you see is to lie to yourself and everyone else so that nobody knows how worthless you feel. It's not a place I want to be ever again.

I never have to go back to the way things were—to the pain, the deception, and chaos of the streets. I know I have my work cut out for me, but as long as I stay plugged in, go to church, and keep doing what I learned here, I can be everything my parents want me to be, everything I want to be now. I know I have a lot to make up for, and I'm willing to put in the work to earn my family's trust again. But today, I am free.

Mike's story is one of hope for his future. His hard work, his parents' years of dedication, his sister's patience and prayers, all had finally paid off. Right in front of their eyes, they were seeing the young man they had imagined he would be one day. Through it all, they didn't give up. Neither did you.

LOOK HOW FAR YOU'VE COME

Congratulate yourself. You may be looking at your addicted loved one a little differently since you first picked up this book. I pray you feel hopeful and empowered to make a difference in your loved one's life. I pray a breakthrough is coming for you and your loved one, leading to a new reality—a healthy, peaceful reality.

Along the journey, you may have felt as though you were walking into the wilderness at times. The terrain was rocky. You struggled to keep your footing and learned new ways to navigate safely through the consequences of your loved one's world of addiction. I've given you a lot of information and I've challenged you, sometimes beyond what you thought you could handle.

But you did handle it. You worked hard, stepped away when you needed to absorb new ways of thinking and behaving, caught your breath, and went back at it with new determination. You've been challenged and tested, and you experienced what seemed to be every emotion at once. But you did it. You're still here, fighting the good fight.

First Timothy 6:11–12 is your mandate: *"Pursue righteousness, godliness, faith, love, steadfastness, gentleness. Fight the good fight of the faith"* (ESV).

THIS ISN'T A ONE-AND-DONE TYPE OF TRAINING.
YOU KNOW THAT ADDICTION'S PATH ISN'T
LINEAR. YOU'VE FOUGHT IN AREAS THAT WILL
NEED DEFENDING AGAIN.

This isn't a one-and-done type of training. You know that addiction's path isn't linear. You've fought in areas that will need defending again. Keep this book handy. Keep your Bible handier. Use them together as a one-two punch against addiction or any other distraction or destruction that tries to take you down. If you need refreshers or a quick reference, revisit the "New Life Success Steps" at the end of each chapter to stay fresh and alert. The enemy hasn't waved the surrender flag. He is still on the move, so don't let your guard down. Refresh your training and renew your resolve.

I came into your life through this book to join you in a battle in which you were entrenched. You were justifiably afraid. Whether a parent, grandparent, spouse, sibling, extended family, child, or close friend, you were desperate and battle-weary. But you dug deep down and found enough hope to take this journey with me.

You may have felt confused in the beginning. You may not have been convinced your loved one had a problem. You may have felt something was off but didn't know what it was. Then, you learned the signs to look for. They were undeniable, providing proof that nearly crushed you at first, then propelled you forward. There were moments of panic, and maybe still are, but you're learning to drive out the panic with a plan. Knowing there's a problem and not doing anything about it isn't your style. You've proven that in your dedication to this training.

You discovered that addiction is a disease caused by choice, and that there is a cure inside the decision to change. But it takes more than sheer determination to get free. This is a spiritual battle that requires a spiritual weapon. As my spiritual father, David Wilkerson, said, "The Holy Spirit is in charge here." Once you saw addiction's cause and what was necessary to eradicate it, you were ready to question your previous ways of combating it.

You learned that some ways of "helping" don't help at all. You saw that rescuing your loved one can enable them to stay in their addiction. Saving them from the natural consequences that could save their lives is a dangerous decision. I'm proud of you for recognizing areas you needed to work on and making those changes. But the enemy isn't going to miss an opportunity to sneak guilt into our minds. He may have made you wonder if your loved one's addiction was your fault. Lies.

You've become a lie detector, learning how to recognize the ways of the enemy so you could take him down. You took charge of what you allowed into your head.

THERE IS HOPE. BREATHE IT IN. YOU ARE BEING TRANSFORMED INTO THE CATALYST FOR TRANSFORMATION IN YOUR FAMILY. YOU NOW KNOW THE TRUTH, THE TRUTH THAT MAKES YOU FREE AND GIVES YOU NO REASON TO HANG ON TO UNPROFITABLE BEHAVIORS AND WAYS OF DEALING WITH THE ADDICTED LIFE.

John Maxwell says, "Encouragement is the oxygen of the soul." There is hope. Breathe it in. You are being transformed into the catalyst for transformation in your family. You now know the truth, the truth that makes you free and gives you no reason to hang on to unprofitable behaviors and ways of dealing with the addicted life.

In Ephesians 4:21–24, the apostle Paul wrote,

Since you have heard about Jesus and have learned the truth that comes from him, throw off your old sinful nature and your former way of life, which is corrupted by lust and deception. Instead, let the Spirit renew your thoughts and attitudes. Put on your new nature, created to be like God—truly righteous and holy. (NLT)

There is power in knowledge. You felt worn down and weak, uncertain and unprepared. You learned to recognize your enemy, identify his plan, and assemble the tools to guard your family against his attack. You discovered the ability to hurl fierce bombs his way, too. Using the Word of God in all its power makes you strong. You are bravely and boldly looking this thing square in the face and rising to the challenge.

Truth leads to freedom.

Denial leads to death.

Keep clinging to truth.

Even if your loved one wasn't ready to see it, your prayer and preparation chiseled away the lies that kept them in the dark. Keep practicing truth love by setting boundaries and standing your ground. Others are watching, too. You impact everyone around you to live a life of freedom without compromise.

You've made some tough choices along the waywardness of addiction. You've been pushed to make some hard calls, uncomfortable and terrifying decisions that may keep your loved one alive long enough to get help. I applaud you for being willing to do whatever it takes to win a good, long, life for your loved one, no matter the cost, even if you had to dial 911.

Family and friends may not have supported you in this endeavor. You may still be on the outs with people in your life because of the stand you took for your loved one. Keep praying for them. Give them this book. God wants to bring your entire family to a healthy place of healing in His love.

The God of miracles transformed my life, and He can transform the life of your loved one and your whole family. Listen to the voice of the Holy Spirit. When you are at a loss for direction and feel turned around, He will settle you. God has a miracle in store for you. He has big plans for your life. He knows your heart's desire.

God knows what you want for your life and the lives of those you love. He wants to give you every good thing. But you must believe it. We don't even have to come up with the faith for trusting on our own. Ask Him for more faith. Ask Him to help you trust Him. Ask the Lord to help you see your loved one whole, healthy, and free from addiction.

YOUR RECOVERY

It is not God's intention for your addict to be the only one who experiences transformation. Throughout this freedom journey, God has been speaking you, too. Take time to talk with Him. You can't call on Him too much. He never gets tired of hearing from you. He never hits the *Do Not Disturb* button, and it never crosses His mind to turn His back on you. I'm talking to you about *you*, now.

You tirelessly sought answers for your addicted loved one. You covered every possible issue and prepared yourself to handle any situation for the benefit of this person. You claimed the promises of God, working on your responses and communication, honing other skills, so you could help your loved one. But it isn't all about them.

God sees you. Just you. He hasn't missed one tear or tantrum. He watched as you gave everything to prove your love for your family. He has seen it all, even the moments when your frustration wore you down and you spoke too quickly, too harshly. He saw it. He understands. And it never crossed His mind to abandon you. Even when you don't think you have anything to offer, He thinks you were worth dying for.

GOD SEES YOU. JUST YOU. HE HASN'T MISSED ONE TEAR OR TANTRUM. HE WATCHED AS YOU GAVE EVERYTHING TO PROVE YOUR LOVE FOR YOUR FAMILY. HE HAS SEEN IT ALL, EVEN THE MOMENTS WHEN YOUR FRUSTRATION WORE YOU DOWN AND YOU SPOKE TOO QUICKLY, TOO HARSHLY. HE SAW IT. HE UNDERSTANDS.

Mother Teresa said, "Give yourself fully to Jesus. He will use you to accomplish great things on the condition that you believe much more in His love than in your weakness."

There it is. We believe more in the power of His love than the limitations of our weakness. Even with everything you've learned and how much you've grown, will you still feel inadequate, tired, or frustrated on this freedom journey? Of course. That's the reality of being human. We will disappoint ourselves. But God doesn't disappoint. Never has, never will. And He continues giving us what we need to grow and change, as long as we accept it.

As a husband and parent, there were times I thought someone in my family needed to change something about their character. God straightened me out. He let me know He was trying to show me the areas in my own life He wanted to refine. His desire is that we never lose sight of the fact that we are human. We are flawed and need to work on improving ourselves before trying to fix anyone else.

When dealing with someone who has an alcohol or drug problem, it's easy to focus on correcting them as we stop seeing to our own needs. You're learning to stop trying to remedy the issues of someone you have no control over while neglecting the person we do have control over—yourself. You are *not* responsible for your loved one's addiction. You *are* responsible for your own attitudes and actions.

In this time we've had together, we've filled our toolbox with clear, concise, and direct ways to handle the task before us. We have discussed how to cope and react properly when we hit bumps in the road. Change is a choice, and we need to learn to celebrate the small accomplishments whenever we can.

Too often, we focus on the negative issues surrounding the loved ones we are trying to reach. Take time to acknowledge the little milestones in them and in each family member. Transformation is a family business.

Your addicted loved one may be asking themselves, *Is there a second chance for me? Do I really have a shot at this?* When they get clear-minded enough to see their behavior and how they've treated the people in their lives, they will wonder, *Will they ever trust me again?* They may think about the life they knew before addiction poisoned their relationships, if they can remember that far back. *Will there ever be a time when things will be good again?*

We can't go back. Things will never be exactly as they were before addiction entered the picture, but they can be better. Adversity can strengthen you. The experience of what you've been through, the fact that you stuck with your loved one and didn't give up, will make your relationship stronger than it was before drugs or alcohol tried to destroy it. But it will take time. Rebuilding trust always does.

You may envision a future without addiction in your lives and, like your loved one, may wonder, *Can things ever be normal again? Will I ever trust them again?*

REMEMBER, YOUR LOVED ONE DOESN'T KNOW YOU ANYMORE, BECAUSE THEY WERE HIGH. AND YOU DON'T KNOW THEM ANYMORE, BECAUSE THEY WERE HIGH. GIVE EACH OTHER SOME SPACE TO FIGURE OUT HOW YOU NOW RELATE TO EACH OTHER. DON'T MAKE BIG PROMISES, BUT HANG ON TO YOUR BIG HOPE.

You have a new normal. It's a good reality. There's been a lot of damage. The worst may be over, but don't ignore the additional healing needed. But again, the reality is that trust takes time.

After your loved one has received the help they need, they will still deal with self-doubt, fear of the future, insecurity, and a lot of regrets. Reentry into the home can bring up difficult memories and insecurities. Your loved one may not know where they fit within the dynamic of the family anymore.

In fact, your family dynamic will change. Many of us have become settled into our familial roles, but addiction alters things. You've all responded to every shockwave of the consequences of your loved one's issues. The family may need to float for a while. Don't push too much. Get to know each other again.

If you are on the other side and your loved one is now a *former* addict, you can shift some of your attention to other areas, including taking care of your own needs. I know how all-consuming the management of addiction's consequences can be. No judgment.

Remember, your loved one doesn't know you anymore, because they were high. And you don't know them anymore, because they were high. Give each other some space to figure out how you now relate to each other. Don't make big promises, but hang on to your big hope. We serve a big God who is in the business of big miracles. If you haven't seen the one you're waiting for yet, keep praying and waiting. You will.

After your loved one finishes their rehabilitation program, watch and see a new creation emerge. The key to sustained growth is connection. No matter how good the curriculum, case management, or mentorship efforts in your program of choice, the long-lasting success and transformation is secured in what happens next. Your loved one must stay plugged in to support. For me, it meant involvement in our church—*really* involved, not just one or two Sundays a month, with Easter and Christmas thrown in. Plugging into a spiritual community is vitally important to the lasting freedom of your loved one.

WHAT'S NEXT?

Now that you are armed with information from this book, it's time to face the problem head on. Resolve, determine that you *will* find a way to help your loved one beat this situation. You will be victorious. It will take a lot of work on your part, along with a great deal of patience.

Continue to remind your loved one of the advantages that come from seeking help, while making your boundaries clear. This is an ongoing battle. Press on, pray for them, and keep the channels of communication open without compromising your convictions and the truth. Remember, your addicted loved one is human. No matter how bad it looks, the more you reach out to them, the greater the chances are that, one day, he or she will see the light. In the meantime, there are things you can do to protect the other people in your life and help prevent them from slipping into addictions or other areas of defeat.

Preventive measures for spouses

+ Renew your love. Look to what first drew you together.

+ Guard against isolating your loved one. This applies to yourself, family, friends, and activities.

+ Celebrate life. Intentionally do things together, except where it is illegal, immoral, or inappropriate.

+ Pray for your spouse daily.

+ Celebrate how God is at work in your relationship and journal your gratitude.

Few people know the pain of loving an addicted spouse. Marriages infiltrated by addiction are infused with anger, betrayal, infidelity, isolation, abandonment, and financial hardship. When addiction enters the relationship, we experience lots of *for worse* with little *for better.*

Addiction makes you a house divided. Your divided house will not stand long-term without the intervention of God. But take heart, because with God, all things are possible.

Preventive measures for children

+ Get involved with your children—their school, sports, friends, entertainment, and most of all, church.

+ Be their hero, not their worst critic.

+ Use love dipped in authority to deal with correction and prevention.

+ Become intentional about laughing with your kids.

+ Don't allow your own guilt to rob your children of your place in their lives. Don't be afraid of push-back. There are times when parents are not the good guys—nor should they be.

+ Time is of the essence. Don't let the window close. Give your children time while you still can.

Preventive measures for other loved ones

+ Stay connected. Use texting, calls, social media, and emails to reach out.

+ Encourage accountability. Find mutual activities you can enjoy together.

+ Invite them to attend healthy environments with like-minded friends.

+ Include them in some of your activities.

But Jesus...answered him, "Do not be afraid any longer; only believe and trust [in Me and have faith in My ability to do this]."

(Luke 8:50 AMP)

Healing is yours for the taking. Reach out, ask God for help, and then receive it. Never lose hope that your loved one will be healed. My life, and the lives of so many others, is proof that God can even bring the dead back to life.

Your loved one was made for more than this. Don't give up!

NEW LIFE SUCCESS STEPS

+ Pray, pray, and then pray some more. And after that, pray.

+ Have faith enough for the both of you. Have faith enough for the whole family if necessary.

+ Keep fighting for your addicted loved one until they can do battle for themselves.

+ Choose to believe beyond what you can see.

+ Picture their future and believe the vision.

+ Celebrate your loved one's freedom—dare to believe!

APPENDIX AND RESOURCES

TREATMENT CONSIDERATIONS

Once you have a list of possibilities, find out what each treatment program offers, and check their program against your needs. As discussed in chapter 12, these are the criteria I suggest your family look for when vetting a program. These considerations are important to your loved one's recovery.

1. Will the program get at the root cause of addiction?

Will this facility deal only with the addiction and its symptoms, or will it help your loved one address the root causes, head-on? Will it dig deep or just put a bandage on the problem? A successful recovery program must deal with the heart, soul, body, and mind. It needs to consider the total person.

2. What is the length of the program?

A short-term program will provide limited effectiveness in preparing your loved one for lifelong sobriety and a drug-free life.

A long-term program on the other hand, gives your loved one the chance to progress through the various levels of surrender required for real change to take place. This is where they will learn to build a new life apart from drugs and alcohol—a lasting life of freedom.

3. How are they prepared for the next stage of their life?

You want them to have the skills necessary when they are released back into the world. Ask the program representative what they offer in the way of education, vocational training, life skills instruction, and career preparation.

Ask if they are taken through the process of writing resumes, conducting job searches, interview preparation, and how to dress for the workplace.

In addition, an addict with children requires parenting classes.

4. Do they offer programs and support for the rest of the family?

Because addiction is a family problem and has likely devastated every member of the household, the entire family needs assistance. When you're researching recovery programs, inquire about what types of family support are offered.

5. How is the addict prepared for the next stage of their life?

Aftercare is a crucial aspect of any recovery program. Find out if this essential element for accountability and support is provided after your loved one has completed treatment.

If treatment is local, your loved one needs face-to-face meetings. If they live far from the facility, they need access to regular support via telephone, online video calls, or even social media.

6. What is the re-entry policy?

What if your loved one graduates, and down the road, stops doing the basics necessary for successful recovery? Although you and your loved one need to understand that re-entry into the facility is not guaranteed when they leave treatment, your loved one can make bad decisions and end up needing help again.

Each treatment center has its own eligibility criteria and usually is decided on a case-by-case basis. Find out what their policy is in the event of relapse.

7. Do your homework.

Google "treatment programs," but look beyond the home page. What are they about? What are their foundational beliefs? Are there endorsements from former participants and their families? Do they have a long track record of success? Have you verified their advertising claims? Are there online reviews or chats you can read through?

For best results, your loved one should enter treatment ready to see it through to the end. This is about setting them up for long-term success by not giving them a way out part-way through their commitment.

If recovery isn't uncomfortable, your loved one isn't doing it right.

Change is hard. But it is possible.

RESIDENTIAL AND GROUP RESOURCES

Keeping the suggested criteria from the previous section in mind, it is up to you to advocate for your addicted loved one. Below are a few suggestions to get you started in your search for a treatment facility that will assist your family in their efforts toward life-long change and freedom. Do your own research, but this should help get you started.

Residential

New Life For Youth (and Adults)—Founded by Victor and Carmen Torres, this faith-based 12-18 month residential program offers help for men and women 18-49 years of age.

Apply online at newlifeforyouth.org_
Call 1-844-231-HOPE (4673)

Teen Challenge—Christ-centered programs for adults & teens, founded by David Wilkerson.

For center locator: https://www.teenchallengeusa.com/
Call (417) 581-2181

Victory Homes International—Faith-based recovery homes worldwide.

For locations— https://victoryhomesinternational.org
Call (909) 599-4437 ext. 135 or 115

Non-Residential

Celebrate Recovery—A Christ-centered 12-step program has meetings in churches, recovery houses, rescue missions, universities, and prisons around the world.

For group locator: https://locator.crgroups.info/

Living Free—Curriculum for individual study and small group support.

https://www.teenchallengeusa.com/about/discipleship/living-free

HOUSE RULES AND AGREEMENTS

These samples are just a guide to help you get started with your own house rules, goal plans, and self-care commitments.

Adjust guidelines to be age and relationship appropriate. Some rules would apply for a parent/child relationship but not for a spousal or friend relationship, for example. Only you can determine what works for your situation.

I suggest that you divide your rules into two categories: negotiable and non-negotiable. If there are conditions that, if your loved one doesn't agree to them, you would not allow them to move in with you, those are your non-negotiables. Other rules can be reviewed and adjusted together with your loved one, but once in place, need to be adhered to until the point that you both agree they aren't necessary.

Timing is important with these contracts. The optimal time to discuss these expectations with your loved one is *before* he or she leaves treatment. I know of one wife who picked her husband up from treatment, drove to their home and sat in the driveway in the car with him and his belongings, refusing to get out of the car until they discussed these expectations. Your loved one needs to know, in very clear terms, what is expected of them and what they can expect from you, to minimize conflicts down the road.

Some of these rules will get more relaxed or even be unnecessary as they get more clean time and you get more confident in who they are becoming. Let your loved one know that the guidelines may seem rigid in the beginning, but trust was damaged and needs time to be rebuilt.

GOALS

Setting goals and forming a plan to achieve them is necessary for success, not just for your loved one, but for everyone. As a part of your Success Strategies, I've included a **Goals and Commitments** list, as well as its partner, your **Goals—Next Steps Planner** to help your loved one and anyone else in your circle to set goals and strategize the specific steps it will take to achieve them.

With the **Goals and Commitments** list, you will document your needs, desires, and commitments in the areas of Sobriety, Family, Work/School, Spiritual, Physical, and Emotional, and I've left you a section for others that don't fall into any of those general categories.

Once those goals are determined, the **Goals-Next Steps Planner** will help you do exactly what the name indicates. You will take each goal from your Plan of Action list and plan out what you will do next to get you closer to your goal. This is where your plan gets activated. On this planner you pull from your general goals and apply specific next steps. You'll include contacts, phone numbers, and any information needed to do the next thing necessary in your quest. Don't worry. I've included an example to give you an idea of how it will work. But this is just an example. You and your loved one will adjust it to fit your needs and situation.

Don't worry if this exercise feels a little awkward at first. Many people have lived a life of "good intentions," without ever seeing them become reality. It's not enough to have an idea of what we want. We have to have a plan and then we have to break it down so that we see what our next step is. And then, we have to actually take that next right step. Hopefully, this tool will help with that process. I want to provide you with the tools you need to enjoy the life God designed for your family.

SAMPLE HOUSE RULES

Living at Home Agreement

We are very proud of the steps you have taken to become the person you were meant to be, and we want to do everything we can to help you achieve your goals in life.

Here are some guidelines so that our home can be a happy, healthy, and whole place for all of us.

These first two are <u>Non-Negotiable</u> terms for your return home:

1. Accept random drug and alcohol tests and provide <u>consent</u> for us to see the results.

2. Follow all recommendations given by treatment facility, including attending weekly support meetings.

These are Basic House Rules for a mutually fair, and respectful coexistence:

+ Sober living. No use of drugs or alcohol. Prescription medications may be monitored for your safety.

+ No smoking in or around the house or in the cars.

+ Obey the law.

+ Adhere to all Probation requirements and keep all appointments.

+ Complete Community Service hours.

+ Go to school, do all homework, etc.

+ Find a job by *(date)* .

+ Begin paying rent/expenses by *(date)*.

+ Any money received will be accounted for weekly. Keep receipts. This is for your protection.

+ Do not carry more than $_____ at any time.

+ Keep a consistent sleep/wake/meal schedule. We want you to be healthy! Sleep by midnight and wake up by 8:00 a.m.

- Be considerate of other people's schedule.

- No friends inside the house or on our property without our presence or approval.

- Be considerate and respectful of others, including their personal property. Ask if you want to use something.

- Speak calmly and quietly. There is no reason for any of us to raise our voices to each other. If you disagree with something, calmly express your opinion, respecting that the final decision may not rest with you.

- Speak politely to and about others.

- No cussing, please.

- Clean up after yourself.

- The doors will be locked at 11:20 p.m. on weeknights and 1:00 a.m. on weekends. If you cannot be home before doors are locked, please let us know where you will be staying before 11:00 p.m.

- Please let us know where you will be and if plans change, so that you keep yourself accountable and we don't worry unnecessarily. There should be no unapproved or unaccounted for time.

- No driving alone without approved accountability

- Do your chores without having to be reminded. We all have to take care of our home.

- If you are tempted to use/drink, let us know so that we can help you. If you slip, tell us. We love you and want to support you but we cannot do that if you're not honest with us.

GOALS & COMMITMENTS

Example

Name: ___Ima Free_____

Date: ___10/17/2018_____

For each of the areas named, list specific goals and commitments, along with due dates where applicable. A more specific breakdown of necessary steps toward achieving these goals can be listed on Next Steps Form.

Sobriety: _Weekly support group meetings; report craving immediately to family or friends; be careful of influences, people, places, things, etc._

Family: _Family night every week; restitution; date night with spouse; time with kids; etc._

Work/School: _Get a jog; get GED; find a tutor, etc._

Spiritual: _Find a church; go to a service every week; read Bible daily; join men's/women's Bible study; connect with small group at church; etc._

Physical: _Eat healthy; get enough sleep and stick to schedule; go to doctor for check-up; make dentist appointment, exercise; etc._

Emotional: _So to counseling; be honest about feelings; etc._

Other: _Contact probation officer; set up community service; pay fines; etc._

GOALS & COMMITMENTS

Name: _____

Date: _____

For each of the areas named, list specific goals and commitments, along with due dates where applicable. A more specific breakdown of necessary steps toward achieving these goals can be listed on Next Steps Form.

Sobriety: _____

_____

_____

Family: _____

_____

_____

Work/School: _____

_____

_____

Spiritual: _____

_____

_____

Physical: _____

_____

_____

Emotional: _____

_____

_____

Other: _____

_____

_____

GOALS: NEXT STEPS PLANNER

Example

Name: Ima Free   **Date:** 12/15/17

Look at your Goals and Commitments list and form a plan, applying specific next steps here. You'll include contacts, phone numbers, and any information needed to do the next thing necessary in reaching your goal.

1. Call Kayla for a ride to Celebrate Recovery: 804-555-1234; delete Facebook account and create a new one

2. Contact Uncle Bruce about plan to repay money for damage to his car; Leave Tuesday night open to go with family to see the *Victor* movie.

3. Call Bill to see about getting my old job back:. 804-555-6321. Plan B: ask Tony from church small group about openings: 804-555-7647. Research where to take practice GED test. Schedule actual GED test

4. Catch a ride with Stacy to Wednesday night's church service. Set alarm to get up earlier to pray and study the Bible before breakfast.

5. Make a meal plan and pre-cook meals for the week. Make doctor appointment Monday: 804-555-4444.

6. Talk to wife about looking for a counselor for us. Do it Saturday before our date night. Discuss with Dad how I felt about the comment he made at dinner. BE RESPECTFUL.

7. Contact probation office Tuesday when she gets back in. Have paperwork in front of me to refer to. Phone number on paperwork. Set up community service with New Life Thrift Store. Call Clerk of Court to find out how much my fines are and make a plan to pay it.

GOALS – NEXT STEPS PLANNER

Name: _____ **Date:** _____

Look at your Goals and Commitments *list and form a plan, applying specific next steps here. You'll include contacts, phone numbers, and any information needed to do the next thing necessary in reaching your goal.*

1. _____

_____

_____

2. _____

_____

_____

3. _____

_____

_____

4. _____

_____

_____

5. _____

_____

_____

6. _____

_____

_____

7. _____

_____

_____

ABOUT THE AUTHOR

Victor Torres was a junkie, drug-pusher, and warlord in Brooklyn's meanest streets. Since his conversion, he has ministered Christ to thousands. He and his wife, Carmen, have traveled to more than thirty nations, preaching the Good News. Their chief undertaking, however, has been New Life For Youth, which began in 1971 in Richmond, Virginia. This growing work is one of the most respected and largest organizations in the country. Today, New Life For Youth has a ranch in Spotsylvania County, Virginia, which is helping an ever increasing number of hurting young men searching for hope, as well as a home for women with drug-related problems called the Mercy House. Their other resources in the Richmond area include House of Hope, a home for recovering men, and Mercy Moms, which serves women and their children.

Victor and Carmen are also the founders and pastors of New Life Outreach International, a fast-growing dynamic church in Richmond, with a congregation spanning more than forty nationalities worshiping together.

In 2017, Victor's life story was made into a major motion picture, *Victor.*